FROM THE TOWER OF BABEL TO ONE WORLD GOVERNMENT

United Nations Against God

Jean-Joseph Boni

Biblical Worldview

biblicalworldview

PREFACE

The emerging New World Order is the overarching development or umbrella under which all the other issues and trends sit - it's the 'bigger picture'. As we move ever closer to the end of the age the New World Order will manifest as the Antichrist's One World Government and Religion (Rev 13). Indeed, with the growing realisation that we're living at the end of the Last Days, it's vital to look at these global issues through an eschatological lens. Their importance is amplified as we appreciate the significance of the trends we highlight on these pages in the light of end time events mentioned in the scriptures.

CONTENTS

THE NEW BABEL

In Genesis 11:1-9, we learn of a united human race, one in both language and purpose, determined to build a tower in the Plain of Shinar. The construction of the tower was to serve as a monument to human achievement. The attitude of the builders was indicative of those who had rejected God as their Creator. Dr. Merrill F. Unger, in his well-known dictionary of the Bible, identifies the basic motivation underlying the entire project as "God-defying disobedience and pride" (Unger's Bible Dictionary, p. 114). In his book, New Age Globalism, H. Edward Rowe wrote:
We must not miss the central warning that resounds through the corridors of the long centuries to our time. The tower builders structured a mighty global organization, independent of God. They dedicated it to the establishment of a human unity which would secure them against the prospect of being scattered apart throughout the world (p. 6).

The Bible, of course, teaches us that God was very much displeased with such an effort, and , as a result, "confounded their language" and "scattered them abroad," the very thing they were trying to prevent!

The New Babel

The descendants of the Babel builders are still with us today. Their plan for creating a "global society" is evident in their various writings. In *Humanist Manifesto II*, under the heading, "World Comworld of barbed wire and concrete block, conflict and cold war. Now, we can see a new world coming into view. A world in which there is the very real prospect of a new world order.... A world where the United Nations, freed from cold war stalemate, is poised to fulfill the historic vision of its founders.

Then, when the wounded dictator of Iraq, a despot we had helped arm, lashed out against people in his own country, we suddenly refused to intervene. Why? We cannot support the Kurds, we were told, because it is not part of the United Nations mandate.

I am not so naive as to think that President Bush allowed himself and Americans to be used by the United Nations. In fact, it is the other way around. Bush effectively manipulated the United Nations apparatus to do what he wanted it to do. We, of course, have strategic interests in this very unstable part of the world, and Saddam Hussein needed to be taught that he could not exercise his military muscle without serious consequences. The military might that was exercised in the Persian Gulf War belonged to America, not the United Nations. The United Nations did what our government wanted it to do, and some will argue that this is good because our cause was just. But, suppose it had not been just? This, of course, is one of the problems with world government. A world government apparatus can be, and eventually will be, used by tyrants and imperialists to manipulate the greater masses for even greater evil. Interestingly enough, Isaiah Bowman, at a U.S. Council on Foreign Relations meeting in May 1942, suggested a United Nations body as a way for the United States to exercise its strength to assure "security" in the world, and at the same time "avoid conventional forms of imperialism" (Memorandum T-A25, May 20, 1942, CFR, *War-Peace Studies*, Hoover Library on War, Revolution, and Peace, Stanford, CA).

Nevertheless, should we not see the irony in an united mankind (viz., the United Nations) in the name of "collective security" assembling once again in the very place where mankind was originally scattered abroad by God because of their ungodly and ill-conceived unity platform?

Globalism And One-World-Ism Is A Man-Made Delusion

The apostle Paul taught a "oneness" of mankind that can only be recognized by those who understand that Jehovah is their Creator (Acts 17:22-31). Nationalism, which has been ordained by the Creator-God, cannot be abridged by man's devices without serious consequences. Ultimately, the solution to mankind's problem is of Divine and *not* man-made origin. All nations are to seek the Lord (Acts 17:26,27). He, and He alone, is the Savior. His house, the church of Christ, has already been established and "all nations [must flow] unto it" in order to be saved (Isaiah 2:2,3). It is only in this everlasting spiritual kingdom that men out of every nation on the face of the earth will "beat their swords into plowshares, and their spears into pruning hooks," and "nation shall not lift up sword against nation, neither shall they learn war anymore" (Isaiah 2:4).

THE MOVE TOWARDS ONE WORLD GOVERNMENT

Interpreting the signs of the times can lead to an accusation that we're simply conspiracy theorists looking for overarching worldviews or answers for why things are like they are. And whilst I endeavour to give evidence for the assertions I make throuhough this essay, there are times when the prophetic scriptures or the person of the Holy Spirit leads us to a specific conclusion that appears contrary to the evidence.

Having said that by way of qualification, I nevertheless think it indisputable that there is a concerted effort amongst the world's elite to create a One World Government; the only real issue at stake is who are they exactly, what methods are they using to achieve their objective, what is their real intent and purpose, is there demonic activity involved and what does God have to say about it.

Recent evidence

Before looking in more detail at the history of this development, I thought we should give a brief overview of some recent evidence.

In 1970 following a call by Nelson Rockefeller for the creation of a New World Order, presidential candidate Jimmy Carter campaigned, saying:

We must replace balance of power politics with world order politics.

Following Desert Storm, President Bush said that the effort was:

To forge for ourselves and for future generations a New World Order . . . in which a credible United Nations can use its . . . role to fulfill the promise and vision of the UN's founders.

Later, when addressing Congress he added:

What is at stake is more than one small country (Kuwait), it is a big idea - a New World Order, where diverse nations are drawn together in common cause to achieve the universal aspirations of mankind . . . Such is a world worthy of our struggle, and worthy of our children's future . . . the long-held promise of a New World Order.

In 1995, the United Nations published a 420 page report: 'Our Global Neighbourhood', which outlined a plan for global governance, advancing the view that nations are interdependent and calling for a strengthened UN. The Report said:

It is our firm conclusion that the United Nations must continue to play a central role in global governance. With its universality, it is the only forum where the governments of the world come together on an equal footing and on a regular basis to try to resolve the world's most pressing problems. Every effort must be made to give it the credibility and resources it requires to fulfil its responsibilities . . . it may serve as the principal mechanism through which governments collaboratively engage each other and other sectors of society in the multilateral management of global affairs.

The Report was vigorously criticized by a number of bodies advocating national sovereignty. By 1996 the term 'global governance' had replaced 'New World Order' in many communications. The thesis advocated not just global governance, but also One World Religion.

In 1999 Tony Blair said:

We are all internationalists now, whether we like it or not.

In 2008 The Financial Times chief foreign affairs columnist Gideon Rachman (who attended the 2003 and 2004 Bilderberg meetings - more on this later) said:

I have never believed there is a secret UN plot to take over the United States . . .but for the first time in my life, I think the formation of some sort of world government is plausible.

In 2009 in the Sunday Times Gordon Brown said it was time:

For all countries of the world to renounce protectionism and to participate in a new international system of banking and regulations to shape the twenty-first century as the first century of a truly global society.

In 2009 in an article in the International Herald Tribune Mikhail Gorbachev said:

Throughout the world there is a clamour for change . . . If current ideas for reforming the world's financial and economic institutions are consistently implemented, that would suggest we are finally beginning to understand the importance of global governance.

Gorbachev's world peace initiatives won him the Nobel Peace Prize in 1990. He's committed to seeing a world government in this century, brought about by manipulating us all into accepting a New

World Order in the guise of saving the planet from environmental catastrophe.

In 1994 he unveiled his plans for his Global Security Programme to the US Council on Foreign Relations. These included a tax on conventional arms production and empowering the UN to fund new UN agencies and authorities which would be part of a New World System. The launch of his programme was basically a world government planning session which was so successful it's now an annual event.

In 2009 former Secretary of State Henry Kissinger (a Rockefeller functionary, member of the Bilderberg group and Trilateral Commission - more on these later) called Obama's election:

An important element in shaping a New World Order.

In an earlier speech he made at a Bilderberg meeting in 1991 in describing how the world could be manipulated into willingly embracing global government he had this to say:

Today Americans would be outraged if UN troops entered Los Angeles to restore order; tomorrow they will be grateful. This is especially true if they were told there was an outside threat from beyond, whether real or promulgated, that threatened our very existence. It is then that all peoples of the world will plead with world leaders to deliver them from this evil. The one thing every man fears is the unknown. When presented with this scenario, individual rights will be willingly relinquished for the guarantee of their well being granted them by their world government.

If the world will not embrace Kissinger's Utopian dream rest assured there is another way - he and his elite entourage will impose it. Slowly but surely they will limit personal freedoms and outlaw opposition. For them, the will to control is all that matters. When you reject God's way and refuse to trust him for the future you have to develop your own peace and security, whereby you remain in control of your own destiny.

The Superclass behind the drive for global governance

Before us lies great uncertainty and a world in flux. We live in an increasingly global village where global solutions to global problems are deemed to be the way forward. At the same time a great consolidation of power is rising of which most people remain unaware. A self-appointed ruling superclass is emerging with a Utopian dream whether we like it or not.

Postmodern, liberal, secular, religious and ideologically driven individuals and groups within the intelligentsia – those who regard themselves as the ruling elite, progressive, open-minded and intellectually and spiritually enlightened, lead and encourage the movement toward a New World Order with the ultimate aim of One World Government.

This elite group includes politicians, world leaders, international bankers and financial institutions, secret societies/organisations, national and international organisations and foundations, multinational companies, non-governmental organisations (NGO's), collegiate fraternities, gentlemen's clubs, think tanks, intelligence agencies, former key political leaders, wealthy oligarchs, New Age devotees, religious leaders and the apostate Church, etc.

The Economist newspaper in 2008 pointed to research by academic David Rothkopf, whose book, Superclass: The Global Power Elite and the World They Are Making, documented how only around six thousand people worldwide actually dictate the majority of policies operating at a global level. The Economist described this comparatively small number of elites as being:

. . . groomed in world-spanning institutions . . . (who) meet at global events such as the World Economic Forum at Davos and the Trilateral Commission or . . . the Bilderberg meetings or the Bohemian Grove seminars that take place every July in California.

Until the late 20th century governments of the great powers provided most of the superclass, accompanied by a few heads of international movements (e.g.the Roman Catholic Church) and bankers (e.g. Rothschild and Rockefeller). In the early 21st century however, economic clout began to rule, fueled by the explosive expansion of international trade, travel and communication.

Today, the nation state's power is diminishing and elected politicians are reduced to minority power brokers. Leaders in international business, finance and the defense industry now dominate the superclass. Although diverse in nature, this network is organised relationally.

Shadow government

It is argued by some that this diverse body already functions unofficially as a relational shadow global government. This is not without foundation since it can be shown that collectively they control political power, international finance, international law, world trade, the media, military capability and religious institutions.

Regional power, the forerunner to global power, is now well established. Few would argue that political and economic power no longer resides with publicly elected representatives, but with powerful individuals and entities exercising control from behind the scenes.

Faceless international elites, organisations and bureaucrats whom we didn't elect now set aside values and traditions we've cherished – the nation-state, democracy and Judaeo-Christian values.

Planetary Utopia or Antichrist's New World Order?

Many amongst this elite operate with sincerity from a genuine conviction that global governance is the answer to the world's ills and so they promote their Utopian agenda openly. Political leaders openly guide their countries down a path of surrendering national sovereignty believing that earthly, planetary Utopia will be the result of One World Government.

Painful years of international conflict, monetary collapse, social unrest and a desire for peace create a catalyst for unthinking acceptance of these Utopian plans - global solutions to global problems are seen as the only solution. As we have already said, when man stops trusting God for the future he inevitably has to find his own solutions - his own Utopia.

At the other end of the continuum however, as I will show, are those who operate from different motives. The Devil promised Adam and Eve that if they ate from the tree of the knowledge of good and evil their eyes would be opened and they would become like God (Genesis 3:5). They have bought into this lie hook, line and sinker. They believe they share divinity and give their allegiance to the one who first told them they could be like God. They serve their father the Devil.

With subterfuge and in secret their demonic agenda is nothing less than to make way for the coming Antichrist's One World Government and Religion. From the prophetic scriptures we know that the Antichrist is set to appear as the dominant political, military and religious figure in the world. They believe that they will share in the reign of Lucifer the light bearer. They have developed a hatred of God the Father and his son Jesus Christ.

In between these two extremes are those (both secular and religious) who simply want worldly wealth, power and control for themselves and will do everything in their power to ensure it is they who ultimately run the global government. They're prepared to use manipulation and intimidation in their personal search for world domination.

Today, these three different groups and variations in between, with their diverse agenda, are happily working alongside each other since for now they are seen to be pushing for the same goal.

The Bible, as we have said, makes it clear that those carrying the Luciferic agenda will initially prevail. Through their wealth and power (both worldly and demonic), their hidden strategy will succeed. Their task, for which they work tirelessly day and night, is to persuade and prepare an unsuspecting world to welcome and accept the Antichrist when he appears.

The anti-Christ will appear as an 'angel of light' and initially be seen as the one who can save mankind. When this happens, we'll all be obliged to use a global e-currency, without which we'll not be able to buy or sell. The 'mark of the beast' will be compulsory.

Life will be controlled by a supreme central power operating out of a world capital city. The once proud nation states will have disappeared and Big Brother will have arrived. Welcome to the future.

Whilst in this chapter I focus on the emerging intellectual, economic and political system, it needs to be understood that this is developing in tandem with the One World Religious system, and that both will be under the control of the Antichrist.

Ancient Babylon

The origins of the drive for global governance, had its roots in the building of the Tower of Babel, where man made his first abortive attempt at global dominance in defiance of God. Man' s first Utopian plan however, proved to be a failure.

Now the whole world had one language and a common speech. As men moved eastward, they found a plain in Shinar and settled there. They said to each other, 'Come, let's make bricks and bake them thoroughly.' They used brick instead of stone, and bitumen for mortar. Then they said, 'Come, let us build ourselves a city, with a tower that reaches to the heavens, so that we may make a name for ourselves and not be scattered over the face of the whole earth.'

But the Lord came down to see the city and the tower that the men were building. The Lord said, 'If as one people speaking the same language they have begun to do this, then nothing they plan to do will be impossible for them. Come, let us go down and confuse their language so they will not understand each other.' So the Lord scattered them from there over all the earth, and they stopped building the city. That is why it was called Babel - because there the Lord confused the language of the whole world. From there the Lord scattered them over the face of the whole earth (Gen 11:1-9)

I believe that it's imperative that we find where we stand within prophetic history. If we can't identify where we are in God's prophetic calender, the events that lie ahead will ambush us, bringing fear and confusion. It's our conviction that this is best ascertained by being in close fellowship with others who share the eschatological hope, and that this must be the backdrop for studying the scriptures.

I believe that there are two major keys to discerning the current prophetic season, one of which is understanding Babylon in the purposes of God both past and future. The other is to understand Jerusalem/Israel in the purposes of God. Israel is said by many to be God's time-clock.

The Bible can be read as the story of two cities - Jerusalem and Babylon. Babylon, both as a city and as a type of society or system, can be found throughout the Bible culminating in End-Time prophecies. We believe that the rebellion led by Nimrod will reach its fulfilment in the coming of the Antichrist. As Babylon rises toward her ultimate expression as Babylon the Great, we can see Satan at work to unify the earth in defiance of God.

The current rise of Postmodernism, sexual immorality and false religion attests that Babylon is soon to reach her final and greatest manifestation. The New World Order comprising One World Government and One World Religion may be closer than we realise.

The Bible refers to Babylon in 18 different books. The longest Old Testament prophecy is the foretelling of Babylon's fall in Jeremiah 50-51. The longest passage of prophecy in the New Testament is John's vision of the great harlot in Revelation 17-18. Babylon is a key biblical theme and according to Peter Herder in his book: 'Babylon,' the Apostle John describes eight characteristics of the coming manifestation:

- She is the originator of false religions
- She is enthroned upon the nations (Rev 17:15)
- She is the centre of global commerce (Rev 18:3)
- She is the ultimate symbol of human rebellion against God (Rev 18:7)
- She intoxicates the nations with sexual immorality (Rev 17:2)
- She persecutes God's saints (Rev 17:6)
- She is empowered by and paves the way for the Antichrist
- Her destruction comes quickly and completely (Rev 18:10)

There are different schools of thought regarding who or what Babylon refers to and I believe that we do not yet have all the information we need to be certain as to how it is all going to pan out. Opinions differ, but most are agreed that Babylon is a symbol of every kind of evil and that it will have demonically-inspired worldwide influence in the areas of politics, economics and religion at the end of the age.

Some Christians consider any connection with the historical city of Babylon to be purely metaphorical. Others however, believe that the ancient city will be rebuilt on its original site on the banks of the Euphrates (some miles away from the modern city of Baghdad) and will become the Antichrist's headquarters - the capital city of the One World Government.

Maybe it's more than coincidental that Saddam Hussein rebuilt the ancient city and had Baghdad's airport renamed 'Babel.' He worshipped Ishtar, Babylon's favourite goddess.

I believe that as the return of Jesus draws closer, more revelation will flow from the Holy Spirit, hence the need to watch and pray. At one level, we will be dealing with a mystery until Jesus returns. However, I do not believe it's unreasonable to anticipate that the One World Government when fully established, will manifest all of the above characteristics. All the evidence points in this direction.

There are many interpretations of what the New World Order will involve, but any or all of the following, in my view, are possibilities:

-   totalitarianism will be the order of the day
-   suppression of dissent and suspension of civil liberties, including free speech
-   internment and/or death of opponents
- enslavement either overtly or covertly of the majority of humanity
-   population control, including a possible culling of the population
-   power in the hands of an elite
-   Satanic worship

We already begin to experience many of these aspects.

Fresh endeavours

Some within society have never lost their demonic lust for global dominance in defiance of the God of the Bible. Down the centuries there have always been individuals, secret societies, global bankers and organisations with a pantheistic, occult, Luciferian agenda wishing to see the Tower rebuilt.

What was conceived in the city of Babel and continued by the Babylonians was revived in Rome (a type of neo-Babylon with the same characteristics) which epitomised the worst excesses of ancient Babylon. The greatest manifestation however, is still to come . . .

ANCIENT SECRET SOCIETIES, BANKERS, WORLD LEADERS, ORGANIZATIONS AND NATIONAL AND INTERNATIONAL INSTITUTIONS

As Babylon rises toward her ultimate expression as Babylon the Great, we can see Satan at work to unify the earth in defiance of God. The current rise of Postmodernism, sexual immorality and false religion attests that Babylon will soon reach her final and greatest manifestation. The New World Order comprising One World Government and Religion may be closer than many realise.

I will discuss further the involvement of the global elite, which includes secret societies, global bankers, world leaders, organisations, and national and international institutions.

I'll show that we're being skillfully manipulated and manoeuvred by powerful Luciferic forces whereby one day in the not too distant future they hope we will welcome and accept Antichrist's One World Government and Religion. Ruthless and conspiratorial secret societies using infiltration techniques, control and intimidation are working for the coming Antichrist and committed to the destruction of Christianity.

Their aim is to bring an end to national sovereignty and to replace Christianity with a pantheistic, occult, mystical, Pagan spirituality which will ultimately lead to the worship of Antichrist and Lucifer. At the heart of the New World Order is an attempt to overthrow God and to replace him with Satan.

I'll also show that this drive for global governance is being controlled and financed by a small number of powerful banking families operating within and through these secret societies. These bankers, between them, hold much of the world's wealth, through which they are able to buy control of the media, manipulate and control world leaders and international organizations.

They seek the creation of new national and international institutions and personally create and fund education and research programmes specifically geared to the promotion of global governance and pantheistic One World Religion. Through their wealth and power they also have the ability to generate violence, instigate wars and chaos, creating fear and a desperate longing for order - their New World Order, their version of Utopia.

What we will be dealing with here in this chapter is unlikely to be found in history text books or mentioned in the mass media, other than when it's denouncing so-called conspiracy theories. But whilst what I write may at times sound implausible, just remember that truth can sound stranger than fiction. This is such a case. The truth is that our history books contain more fiction than fact, if the truth be told.

Secret societies

Secret societies are as old as human culture. With religion came spirituality, mysticism, knowledge of the world of spirits and otherworldly powers; the kind of knowledge that humans have sought to keep secret believing it gives them power over others.

The earliest secret societies have their roots in pre-history and from these primitive roots a long tradition stretches down through time. Where prehistory shades into ancient history, it's possible to catch the first glimpse of this tradition in the form of the mystery religions and the ancient gods of Sumer, Egypt, Greece and Rome.

Freemasons claims that there is a direct line of decent from the ancient mysteries to Freemasonry and there are certainly many parallels between the movements. The societies known as Knights Templar and the Illuminati come into this category .

In the last century or so a number of modern secret societies have been created, including the Council on Foreign Relations, the Tri-lateral Commission, the Bilderbergers, Skull and Bones, etc. Whenever something has to remain hidden in order to hide the real intent of its members, a new society is often seen as the answer.

These societies, ancient and modern, have had a profound impact on the course of history and continue to do so. I'll show in this series of articles that they are the energy behind the push for the creation of a New World Order and the coming Antichrist.

The 19th century British Prime Minister Benjamin Disraeli, recognising their influence and power, said:

The world is governed by very different personages from what is imagined by those who are not behind the scenes (1844).

There is in Italy a power which we seldom mention in this

House . . . I mean the secret societies . . . It is useless to deny, because it is impossible to conceal, that a great part of Europe – the whole of Italy and France and a great portion of Germany, to say nothing of other countries – is covered with a network of these secret societies, just as the superficies of the earth is now being covered with railroads (1856).

The government of this country has not only to deal with governments, kings and ministers, but also with secret societies, elements which must be taken into account, which at the last moment can bring our plans to naught, which have everywhere their unscrupulous agents, who incite assassinations and can if necessary lead a massacre (1876).

Serious words indeed. President John F. Kennedy was also well aware of the control exercised by America's secret societies and his many perceived rebellious decisions against the global elite, could ultimately have led to his assassination. In 1961, in an address to newspaper publishers, he said:

The very word 'secrecy' is repugnant in a free and open society, and we are as a people, inherently and historically, opposed to secret societies, secret oaths, and secret proceedings . . . For we are opposed around the world by a monolithic and ruthless conspiracy that relies primarily on covert means for expanding its sphere of influence.

It depends on infiltration instead of invasion, on subversion instead of elections, on intimidation instead of free choice. It is a system which has conscripted vast human and material resources into the building of a tightly knit, highly efficient machine that combines military, diplomatic, intelligence, economic, scientific, and political operations.

Its preparations are concealed, not published, its mistakes are buried, not headlined, its dissenters are silenced, not praised, no expenditure is questioned, no secret is revealed . . . I am asking your help in the tremendous task of informing and alerting the American people.

Unfortunately, the media was already controlled by the secret societies and bankers and so this message was largely curtailed. Increasingly, students of the Kennedy assassination are coming to believe that his opposition to the globalists' agenda may have played a significant factor in his unsolved death.

The Masonic Jewish connection

We're often asked how Jewish financiers became linked with secret societies and a Luciferic agenda. The answer, I believe, is quite simple and relates to their involvement in the practice of Kabbalah. Kabbalah means 'traditions containing hidden messages' and is a form of Gnosticism. It is in essence pantheistic, esoteric and occult. Kabbalists believe in the non-existence of evil and in the deification of man. It is thought to be of Jewish origin.

Coded knowledge was thought to be found within the Torah and other old Hebraic texts such as the Sefer Yezirah (Book of Creation) and the Sefer HaZohar (Book of Light). According to the Book of Light 'mysteries of wisdom' were given to Adam by God whilst in the Garden of Eden. These secrets were then passed on through Adam's sons to Noah and then on to Abraham. Abraham is said to have possessed a tablet of symbols representing all of the knowledge of human kind handed down from the time of Noah.

This was known to the Sumerians (Abraham hailed from Sumer) as the Table of Destiny and to the early Jews as the Book of Raziel. It reportedly provided King Solomon with his wisdom. The Table of Destiny was also known to Greek and Roman masters such as Homer, Virgil, Pythagoras, Plato and Ovid. Moses, it is said, had learned the mysteries whilst he was in Egypt.

These books predate the Talmud - the Talmud (612 laws) was developed by the Rabbis who had been exiled to Babylon (around 586 BC) by Nebuchadnezzar; because they no longer had a Temple or land they began to write down the Mosaic law which the Talmud expanded and explained in minute detail.

The Jews that Jesus claimed were of their father the Devil (Jn 8:44) were Kabbalah Jews. Babylonian, Talmudic Pharisaism taught traditions based on the Talmud and Kabbalah and not on the law of Moses. The Talmud contradicts the whole spirit of Moses.

When, in the 1st Century AD, the Council of Jamnia was convened to redefine Judaism following the destruction of Jerusalem in 70 AD - once again there was no temple, no blood sacrifice and therefore no means for forgiveness of sins - they turned to Kabbalah and to 'good works' based on the Talmud to define who they were. Gnostic, Kabbalah Judaism gained ground, whilst Mosaic Judaism lost ground.

The mystical knowledge of the Kabbalah passed from Mesopotamia through Palestine into medieval Europe, where it first appeared in writing at the end of the 13th century. A Spanish Jew named Moses de Leon wrote it down.

The Knights Templar brought Kabbalah to Europe from the Holy Land at the time of the Crusades, and the esoteric knowledge was developed through an alliance of the Knights Templar and Masonic guilds. Masonic historians acknowledge that the first evidence of 'Judaeo-Christian mysteries' introduced into Freemasonry came about during this time.

It's well documented that Kabbalah was utilised by nearly all the secret societies including Freemasonary, Rosicrucianism and Illuminism right through to the modern societies. Most Jews today are unaware that Judaism largely rejects the Old Testament in favour of the Talmud and Kabbalah.

Kabbalah is the basis of modern witchcraft, astrology, numerology, tarot cards, black magic, androgyny, sex worship and much of the New Age Movement.

Moses Mendelssohn, a noted Jewish philosopher who did much to liberate Jews from repressive German laws, was a Jewish Kabbalist and mentor of Illuminati founder Adam Weishaupt. Here we begin to make the link between a Jewish banker and the secret societies.

Mendelssohn is likely to have been the link between Weishaupt and banker Mayer Rothschild (a Jew). Another link may also be Michael Hess, the tutor of Rothschild's children and a follower of Mendelssohn, who later headed the Philanthropic School for needy Jewish children established by Rothschild.

Although Illuminati concepts can be traced back through history to the earliest sects claming esoteric knowledge, the order was first publically identified in 1776. In that year the Masonic hierarchy created a new ultra-secret society, the Illuminati, from within Free-masonry. This was founded in Bavaria by Adam Weishaupt, a pro-fesser of Canon Law at Ingolstadt University in Bavaria, Germany, with the specific occult Luciferian agenda to establish a New World Order.

One of his cofounders reportedly was William of Hesse, the em-ployer of Mayer Rothschild. Weishaupt was devoted to the ancient mysteries of Mesopotamia shown by the fact that he had the Illu-minati adopt the Persian calendar.

According to Jim Marrs in his book:' Rule by Secracy,' unlike an-archists that seek an end to all government, Weishaupt and his Il-luminati sought a world government based on their philosophy of human-centred rationalism. This world government, of course, would be administered by themselves. Weishaupt said:

The pupils (of the Illuminati) are convinced that the order will rule the world. Every member therefore becomes a ruler.

The order developed lodges in many European nations and by 1782 it was recognised amongst Europe's occultists as the undisputed leader of the occult, One-World Movement. It comprised an inner circle of illumined or high ranking Freemasons including bankers and their mandate to create a New World Order was to be achieved by influencing the key decisions of Europe's leaders through a process of infiltration.

According to Gary Kah in his book: 'En Route To global Occupation,' this agenda was divulged at the Masonic Conference of Wilhelmsbad in 1782, which drew together representatives of all the Secret Societies (Martinists, Freemasons and Illuminati). It was also decided at this conference to move the headquarters of the Illuminati to Frankfurt, the stronghold of Rothschild and other international bankers.

Weishaupt forged a deal with the growing Rothschild banking empire, thus financing the Order's ambitions. According to Edith Starr Miller in her book: 'Occult Theocracy,' Rothchild's syndicate included Jewish financiers such as Daniel Itzig, Friedlander, the Goldsmiths and Moses Mocatta. Freemasons soon had the banking pre-eminence of their predecessors, the Knights Templar, and the Illuminati grew, attracting royals, nobles and Jesuits across Europe.

Kabbalistic Jewish bankers (many of whom may by now have forsaken their Jewish roots) in amassing their fortunes, found concord within secret societies. Membership of the society provided helpful networks and opportunities for both wealth and power expansion.

According to Miller, the goals of the Illuminati included, amongst other things, the destruction of Christianity, monarchies and nation states. It also sought the abolition of family ties and marriage by means promoting homosexuality and promiscuity. Masons Albert Pike, Manley P Hall, Madame Blavatsky, amongst others, claim that Freemasonry emerged from Kabbalah and would readily identify with and endorse this agenda.

There's a clear link therefore between Jewish occult and the secret societies and between the global Kabbalistic Jewish financiers and the societies. The history of Freemasonry is the history of organised pantheistic occultism and Albert Pike, leading Freemason from 1859-1891, in his Freemasonry manual: 'Morals and Dogma,' traces its origins back to ancient Babylon.

On a point of interest, the Hasidic Jews, many of whom were murdered in the Holocaust, were Kabbalah Jews.

Freemasonry in the US

By the late 1700's, Freemasonry and the Illuminati had a strong foothold in the US. The first Supreme Council of Scottish Rite Freemasonry was established in Charlestown, South Carolina in 1801. It was later relocated in Washington DC and is today the Mother Supreme Council of the World. As the US grew as a world power, the focus of the New World Order proponents moved from Europe to America.

Global bankers and their influence

The European bankers were at the heart of this transition and were not always popular with the politicians. Thomas Jefferson one of the Founding Fathers, the principal author of the Declaration of Independence and the third President of the United States, said:

I believe that banking institutions are more dangerous to our liberties than standing armies.

He has been shown to be right. Money alone has never been

enough to quench the thirst and lusts of the super-rich. They use their unbelievable wealth to achieve power for themselves. Power of a magnitude never before even dreamed of. Tyrants and despots of yesteryear would drool in envy at what is possible today - power on a global scale. Power to control the world ready for the coming Antichrist's New World Order.

For the purpose of this article we will focus on three prominent banking families - the Rothschilds, Rockefellers and Morgans and we will discuss the establishment of the most powerful and secretive financial cartel the world has ever known through which they, with other international bankers, control America's financial activity - some would argue for their own benefit - we speak of the Federal Reserve System.

First let's look at the bankers:

Rothschild

The name Rothschild is synonymous with international banking and can be found behind the scenes in many major world events. This secretive banking dynasty was begun by Mayer Amschel Bauer who was born in 1744. He studied to become a Rabbi, but on the death of his father he became an apprentice in a banking house.

He became court financial agent to William IX a royal administrator of the Hesse-Kassel region and a prominent Freemason. Mayer was also a Freemason and it was during this period that the metaphysics of the Kabbalah began to fuse with Freemasonry.

One of Mayer's clients was the royal German family of Thurn and Taxis, a descendant of which would be executed as a member of the secret society which created Adolf Hitler. Biographer Niall Ferguson said:

From the earliest days, the Rothschilds appreciated the importance of proximity to politicians, the men who determined not only the extent of budget deficits but also the domestic and foreign policies . . . Rothschild influence extended to royalty as well.

The passion for money and power drove Mayer and he launched his global banking operation. He established his son Nathan as head of the London branch and it was around this time that he changed his name from Mayer to Rothschild, which literally means 'red shield.'

From influential yet small beginnings in Germany, the link with secret societies enabled them to expand their banking expertise into much of Europe. Freemasonry provided the international and political contacts they needed and they in turn provided finance for the Freemasonry vision for a New World Order.

By the 19th century, Rothschild was the dominant banking family in Europe and soon turned their eye to America. Their primary link was through the Warburgs of Germany who were partners in Kuhn, Loeb & Co, in New York. Thus Rothschild and the masonic influence began to gain a foothold in the US.

Between 1865 and 1913 the London based Rothschild bankers used agents such as J P Morgan and J D Rockefeller to gain control of American industry and when in 1913 the US Government devolved monitory control to a number of international bankers when they created the Federal Reserve System (more on this later), they included the Rothschild Banks of London and Berlin.

Intermarriages between the prominent Jewish immigrant families were common around the turn of the century. History professor Howard M Sachar wrote:

As they set about protecting their vast estates, moreover, these Jewish dynasts often found it useful in the United States as in Western Europe to marry among each other.

According to Jim Marrs in his book: 'Rule by Secrecy':

Unrelenting attention to business, coupled with intermarriages and the use of front men, built a gigantic and secretive Rothschild banking empire. This empire exerted considerable influence on the economic and hence the political history of Europe as well as the United States, although here (the US) in a more covert and indirect manner.

By 1815 Nathan had become the principal financier to the British Government and the Bank of England.

Rockefellers

Walter Cronkite said:

The Rockefellers are the epitome of the nation's permanent establishment; governments change, economics fluctuate, foreign alliances shift - the Rockefellers prevail.

John Davison Rockefeller Sr, is possibly the most well known rich man in the world even though he's been dead since 1937. No family in America has assembled such power and influence as the Rockefellers thanks to their vast wealth and ties with England and the Rothschilds.

Rothschild finance backed the Rockefeller Standard Oil dynasty, the Carnegie steel empire and the Harriman railroad system. Shortly after the turn of the century, Rockefeller became America's first billionaire.

By the time of his death Rockefeller and his son John D Rockefeller Jr., had not only built up a vast oil empire (by 1880 Rockefeller owned or controlled 95% of all oil produced in the US), but had established such institutions as the University of Chicago (est. 1889), the Rockefeller Institute for Medical Research (est. 1901), the General Education Board (est. 1903), the Rockefeller Foundation (est. 1913), the Lincoln School (est. 1917, where the Rockefeller children began their education) and the Rockefeller University in New York City.

The Rockefellers have used economic power to build political power. Some of these organisations, although very influential in government, are virtually unknown to the average citizen. You will hear them cited by the media as a source for an important opinion about some national or international event.

The Rockefellers are also interested in the eugenics movement, a programme of scientifically applied genetic selection to maintain and improve 'ideal' human characteristics including birth and population control. The Rockefellers created the Population Council, a centre concerned with overpopulation and family planning.

The Rockefellers intermarried with the Carnegies and later financed many US capitalists through Chase Manhattan and Citibank. By the mid 20th century many of the wealthiest families in the US were related to the Rockefellers and much of America's wealth, therefore, can be traced to the old money of Europe and to Freemasonry.

David Rockefeller the youngest son of John D Rockefeller Jr., earned a B.S. degree from Harvard and then entered the London School of Economics, a school largely funded by the Rockefeller Foundation. Here he came into contact with the teachings of Ruskin and other socialists. According to Gary Allen, in 1973 alone, he met 27 heads of state, including the rulers of Russia and China.

The Rockefellers Brothers Fund currently chaired by Steven C Rockefeller makes donations to a Buddhist Zen Centre, Planned Parenthood and groups concerned with environmental issues.

The One World outlook of the Rockefellers is still evident in the Funds 1997 annual report. Abbey M O'Neill, who Steven Rockefeller replaced as chairman, wrote that the Fund had:

. . . a refocused 'One World' strategy, with an explicitly global perspective and an emphasis on the convergence of national and international frameworks.

David Rockefeller, one of the owners of the Federal Reserve Bank, in his 'Memoirs' calls for the end of the sovereignty of the United States while forming a One World Government. Paul Warburg, another founder of the Federal Reserve, has said:

We will have a world government whether you like it or not. The only question is whether that government will be achieved by conquest or consent (February 1950 in testimony before the US Senate).

Over the years, various high-ranking individuals have attempted to expose the work of the Federal Reserve System and the drive of the Rockefellers and their allies to create a One World Government under their control (more on this later).

Education is the primary means for getting the masses to imbibe a new worldview. Knowing this, from the beginning of the 20th century the Rockefellers sought to influence education. Gary Allen in 'The Rockefeller File' says

The foundations (principally Carnegie and Rockefeller) stimulated two-thirds of the total endowment funding of all institutions of higher learning in America during the first third of this century. During this period the Carnegie-Rockefeller complex supplied 20% of the total income of colleges and universities and became in fact, if not in name, a sort of US Ministry of Education.

The Rockefellers also substantially funded John Dewey, the confirmed atheist and 'father of progressive education.' He taught four of the five Rockefeller brothers, including David and Nelson, but spent most of his life teaching teachers while he was Head of Department at Columbia University.

The Reece Commission said that Rockefeller money and Dewey educational philosophy were responsible for:

. . . nurturing some of the most ardent academic advocates of upsetting the American system and supplanting it with a Socialist state.

The chief US education lobby, the National Education Association (NEA) was sponsored by Rockefeller-Carnegie finance, and by 1934 had adopted his philosophy of humanism, socialism and globalism and was actively sowing these in the classroom.

Rockefeller's money was also responsible for creating textbooks which undermined patriotism and free enterprise and for producing study documents for educators promoting a global view of society.

Morgans

According to Jim Marrs the Morgan banking empire continues to hold sway over both business and political decisions being made today, and many Morgan employees and agents can be counted among the membership of the secret societies. The Morgan Company has became one of the most powerful banking houses in the world.

The Morgans acted as agents for the Rothschilds; they were in effect a covert American front for the Rothschilds. Although J P Morgan was born in America in 1856 he traveled to Germany where he studied at the University of Gottingen a hotbed of anti-establishment and secret society activity.

Although J P Morgan and John D Rockefeller competed with each other in many areas, they nevertheless worked together to create the Federal Reserve System. The initial plan for the Federal reserve system was conceived at a secret meeting in 1910 at Morgan's private resort on Jekyll Island of the coast of Georgia.

The Federal Reserve System

In America the ultimate control of money rests with the bankers of the Federal Reserve System. Anyone looking to prove the existence of conspiracies in America need look no further than the origin of the 'Fed' as it has become known.

Seven men attended the initial week-long meeting on Jekyll Island to prepare plans for banking reform following a series of financial panics, some would say which they created. Between them they probably owned a quarter of the world's wealth and the meeting was so secret that only their first names were used.

The Federal Reserve Act was signed into being in December 1913. Today the Fed is composed of 12 Federal Banks, each serving a section of the country, but dominated by the New York Federal Reserve Bank. Despite the word Federal in its name the Fed is not part of the US Government.

Unknown to many, the Fed is a privately owned organization and driven by a vision for One World Government. Its monetary policy decisions do not have to be approved by the President or anyone else in the executive or legislative branches of government. Until a couple of decades ago, the names of the owners were kept a closely-guarded secret.

Other bankers involved in the Federal Reserve System included Lazard Brothers Banks of Paris; Israel Moses Seif Bankers of New York; Kuhn, Loeb Bank & Co. New York; Chase Manhattan Bank of

New York and Goldman, Sachs Bank of New York.

A Fed publication in 1963 states that the function of the Fed is to foster a flow of money and credit that will facilitate orderly economic growth, a stable dollar, and long run balance in our international payments.

I will show that there are major built-in flaws with the Fed from the way in which it was set up, right through to the way it operates today. Charles Lindbergh Sr.,recognised this at the time the Federal Reserve Act was in the process of being passed. He warned:

This Act establishes the most gigantic trust on earth. When the President signs this bill the invisible government of the Monetary Power will be legalised . . . the worst legislative crime of the ages is perpetrated by this banking and currency bill.

However you look at the Fed, at the very least there exists a major conflict of interest. The banker's own financial, Utopian dreams and other interests are so closely intertwined with matters of public policy, both domestic and foreign, that virtually every major government decision affects their financial empire, Utopian vision and other interests in some way. They would have to be saints, which they certainly are not, to always act in the best interest of the Government of America.

The cozy relationships that exist between themselves and those exercising political power make it nigh impossible for them to serve the interests of the people as a whole. Whilst having great wealth should not be an obstacle to power or holding high office, that only works if business stays out of government and government stays out of business, but of course we know that this doesn't happen.

When you also control the media you edge toward the situation where 'Power tends to corrupt and absolute power corrupts absolutely.' This is precisely the situation that exists in the US today. We have a major problem when absolute power seeks to outwork a Luciferic Utopian dream.

The Fed has effectively given financial and political control to the global banking elite, enabling the agenda of the ancient secret societies (Freemasonry, Rosicrucianism, Illuminati, etc) for a pantheistic New World Order to be realised.

Not surprisingly, over the years a number of conservative congressional leaders have endeavoured to expose the operations of the Fed. During the 50's Congressman Reece headed what became known as the Reece Committee, which conducted a thorough investigation into the major tax-exempt foundations linked to the international money cartel.

The Committee discovered that vast profits from public US bank loans were ploughed into Federal Reserve initiatives. By probing into the Rockefeller-based initiatives, the Reece Committee discovered that the true agenda of the recipients was preparation for a 'one-world society.' The Fed had in-roads into all areas of life, but the area of foreign affairs was the most affected.

Rene Wormser of the Reece Committee stated that the influence of the major foundations had 'reached far into government, into the policy-making circles of Congress and into the State Department.' He said:

This has been effected through the pressure of public opinion, mobilised by the instruments of the foundations; through the promotion of foundation-favourites as teachers and experts in foreign affairs; through a domination of the learned journals in international affairs; through frequent appointment of foundation officials to State Department jobs (Wormser: Foundations – Their Power and Influence (1958)).

Wormser also discovered that US foreign policy was shaped by an alliance with the Cecil Rhodes institution. Rhodes, the famous British industrialist after whom Rhodesia was named, was a close ally of Rothschild and European Freemasonry who made his fortune in the diamond mines of South Africa. He used his immense wealth to promote the cause of world government.

After his death, the Rhodes Scholarship Programme continued the global agenda and Rhodes scholars have, and still do, hold many highly influential posts in education, government and media in the US. At the time of the Reece Committee investigations, the president of the Rockefeller Foundation, the director of the Guggenheim Foundation and the former president of the Carnegie Foundation were all Rhodes scholars.

The wealth, power and influence enjoyed by these international bakers means that they are in a position to control the media, stop and start wars, manipulate stock markets, maintain class distinctions and censor the news. They have called for the establishment of regional and global institutes (European Union, League of Nations and the United Nations, etc) including providing land or financial assistance as it was required.

To cover their tracks they have also created a number of modern secret societies (the Club of Rome, Trilateral Commission, Council on Foreign Relations, Bilderbergers, Skull and Bones, etc) to further their aims and to keep their true agenda secret.

THE CONTEMPORY MOVE TOWARDS ONE WORLD GOVERNMENT

In 2000 United Religions Initiative was officially launched. The brainchild of Bishop William Swing in 1993, following an invitation to hold a large interfaith service to mark the 50th year of the signing of the UN charter, it was meant to be a parallel organisation to the UN, and there is a very close connection between them. The home page of the web site (www.uri.org) states:

URI is a global grassroots interfaith network that cultivates peace and justice by engaging people to bridge religious and cultural differences and work together for the good of their communities and the world.

The action areas include peacebuilding, youth, environment, women and global advocacy. The launch ceremony in San Francisco in 2000 began with an occult ritual.

Hans Kung, a Swiss Catholic priest who has been President of the Foundation for a Global Ethic since 1995 said this in relation to the URI:

Any form of church conservatism is to be rejected. To put it bluntly no regressive or repressive religion, whether Christian, Islamic,

Jewish or of whatever provenance has a long term future. If ethics is to be for the long term good of all, it must be indivisible. An undivided world increasingly needs an undivided ethic. Postmodern men and women need common goals, ideals, values, visions. What we need is an ecumenical world order.

Robert Muller, the educationalist pushing the global agenda through national and global curriculum and a keynote speaker at the URI had this to say:

Do not worry if not all religions join the United Religions Initiative. Many nations did not join the UN and later regretted it and made every effort to join. It was the same with the EC and it will be the same with the URI because whoever stays out will sooner or later regret it.

Millennium summit of religious leaders

In August 2000, Kofi Annan, then Secretary-General of the UN, called together 1000 religious leaders in New York. He was strongly supported by Maurice Strong, a key player in the UN Environmental Programme, and sponsored by Ted Turner (media mogul and environmentalist, now the Chairman of the UN Foundation board of directors). The aim was to get the delegates to sign an interfaith declaration that their religion was not the only way to God. Many, but not all, did.

Earth Charter

In September 2000, two events took place in New York – the UN summit and former USSR leader Mikhail Gorbachev's State of the World Forum. Many heads of state attended both. The Summit was attended by 80% of the world's leaders, an unprecedented number. Several treaties were ratified, of the thousands necessary to ensure a world government.

At Gorbachev's Forum which was designed to bring together economic, media and political leaders for global governance, he strongly pushed the implementation of the Earth Charter, which he and Maurice Strong had worked on since the Rio de Janeiro Earth Summit in 1992. It was described by Gorbachev as a 'ten commandments for the environment' and by Strong as 'a Magna Carta for the earth', and had as its preamble:

We stand at a critical moment in Earth's history, a time when humanity must choose its future. As the world becomes increasingly interdependent and fragile, the future at once holds great peril and great promise. To move forward we must recognize that in the midst of a magnificent diversity of cultures and life forms we are one human family and one Earth community with a common destiny. We must join together to bring forth a sustainable global society founded on respect for nature, universal human rights, economic justice, and a culture of peace. Towards this end, it is imperative that we, the peoples of Earth, declare our responsibility to one another, to the greater community of life, and to future generations

The Earth Charter was finally ratified in 2003, financed throughout by Rockefeller money. The state of the environment is the major plank in bringing together all the strands in the push for global governance, since if, as they purport, global warming is so bad, we need a world government to solve the problem; similarly a world government will keep world peace. This is the essence of Gorbachev's initiative, Green Cross International.

Meeting of the World Parliament 2000

Political, religious and environmental elements clearly overlap in the vision for the new world order. In November 2000, Pope John Paul II called together religious and state leaders in Rome. Five thousand politicians from 94 countries came, including Gorbachev by personal invitation of the Pope. The role of both Gorbachev and the radical environmental movement, and the Vatican and its role in interfaith dialogue and the political union of Europe are strategic in all efforts toward global governance.

Since 2000, the planks in the New World Order strategy have moved apace, oiled by the explosion in information technology, the propaganda surrounding global environmental issues such as global warming, and the surge of neo-pagan spirituality. Just in the UK, by way of example, we've seen Judaeo-Christian values increasingly marginalised and ungodly legislation on the increase, whilst more and more of our sovereignty has been given away to Europe. The introduction of the Euro in 2002 and the rapid increase in nations applying for EU membership around that time gives us some clue as to the speed with which regional (and similarly, global governance) can change.

Developments in the World Constitution and Parliament Association (WCPA)

Founded in 1986, it has gathered strength and is still very active, despite the death of its founder, Philip Isely, in 2010, as we shall see.

The home page of the WCPA web site (www.worldparliament-gov-.org) tells us:

The WCPA is a worldwide organization working with love and dedication for planetary peace, justice, freedom, and sustainability. We are widely affiliated with human rights organizations, environmental organizations, peace organizations, and others working for a decent future of planet Earth.

The World Constitution and Parliament Association is the organization responsible for drafting the Constitution for the Federation of Earth and for promoting its ratification by the people and nations of Earth. The WCPA is also responsible for holding sessions of a provisional World Parliament, and for the convening of a Founding Ratification Convention, to obtain official ratification of this Earth Constitution under the criteria given in Article 17 of the Constitution.

The president of the WCPA is now Dr Glen T Martin, and the web site indicates that it is responsible for the Provisional World Parliament, held in India. The 13th session is due to be held at the World Unity and Convention Centre in December 2013.

The affiliated web sites (www.worldproblems.net ; www.radford.edu/gmartin ; www.earthfederation.info ; www.preventplanetarydeath.org) give us a picture of the planetary Utopia the world parliament is striving for, based on a humanistic one world government promoting a one world religion of peace and harmony.

9/11 and increase in terrorism

Meanwhile, in the last decade we saw other developments which indicate that world government is not far away. The events of 9/11, and terrorism since that time, are enough to convince many that a global solution is the only way to make the world a safe place.

United Nations

In 2002, Switzerland became the last country on earth to become part of the UN. (Vatican City is not part; nor is Kosovo a full member.) In effect, the UN at that point became a type of limited world government.

In the same year, meetings took place to strategise the military of the UN, NATO, EU, etc.

International Criminal Court 2002

Pessimists thought it would take twenty years to accomplish the establishment of an International Criminal Court, when the UN first proposed the idea. In fact it took just four years. It is a permanent tribunal to prosecute individuals for genocide, crimes against humanity, war crimes and the crime of aggression (although it cannot, until at least 2017, exercise jurisdiction over the crime of aggression). Eventually its jurisdiction will be extended to cover all kinds of international issues.

The role of the Vatican

In 2002, Pope John Paul II invited world religious leaders to Rome in an effort to promote unity among the religions of the world. Behind this move was the Lucis Trust (founded by Alice Bailey) and other members of theosophical societies. Rooted in the occult, their given agenda was to finally break the Middle East log jam through religious tolerance. They failed in that attempt, but in other respects worldwide religious unity was strengthened.

This move came on the back of significant initiatives years beforehand, in particular Vatican II, which in 1962 encouraged cooperation with Buddhism, Hinduism and other world religions. They established the Secretariat for Non Christians at that time, which would eventually be renamed the Secretariat for World Religions. In the same time span, many protestant churches have made moves toward their Catholic neighbours and a large amount of co-operation now takes place.

Then in 1986, Pope John Paul II called the world religious leaders together in Assisi and they prayed to the 'one god' – the first time this had been done on such a scale and with the Pope leading the prayers.

Another milestone was the 1993 Parliament of the World's Religions in Chicago, where all religions including snake charmers, Wiccans, Voodoo, etc were invited and where the creation of an international religious authority aimed at unifying all of the world's faiths and spiritual traditions was called for. The result was the United Religions Initiative mentioned above.

The Ark of Hope

The Earth Charter document, 'an international peoples treaty for building a just, sustainable and peaceful global society in the 21st century' is housed in what is known as the Ark of Hope, alongside the Temenos Books, which are images and words for global healing, peace and gratitude, based on the philosophy of Carl Jung. The sixteen commandments within it, if obeyed, would, it is said, cure the condition of mankind. The Ark has some similarities to the Ark of the Covenant made by the Israelites. Ceremonies and events where the Ark of Hope features are full of New Age rhetoric. It was housed in the UN Headquarters before going to South Africa.

The Ark of Hope web site encourages communities around the world to share the vision:

The Ark of Hope carrying the vision of the Earth Charter belongs to Earth and humankind. Its life grows when it is shared. It is hoped that nations around the world will bring the Ark to their people, continuing to introduce the Earth Charter to audiences globally, spreading hope and the recognition of the interdependence of justice, and economic and ecological integrity that together build a culture of peace.

World Council of Churches/Vatican Code of Conduct 2008

Let's move forward a few years. The WCC, mentioned in Part .... has as one of its stated aims recognition of the importance of interreligious dialogue and relations with other faiths. From its inception it had the New World Order as its goal but realised that only when Christians were unified would they be in a position to blend with all the other world religions. Thus the WCC set about unifying

Christians around humanistic aims.

The WCC met with the Vatican in 2008 to discuss a protocol on proselytising, an important issue for the Roman Catholic Church particularly in South America where many Catholics were converting to evangelical Christianity. The outcome of the meeting was an agreed 'global code of conduct' whereby food aid, physical support and social aid could be exchanged, but not religion.

UN Alliance of Civilisations

The UNOAC is an initiative proposed by the Prime Minister of Spain, Jose Luis Rodriguez Zapatero at the UN in 2005 and co-sponsored by the Turkish Prime Minister, Recep Tayyip Erdogan. It was designed to prevent international terrorism by forging international, intercultural and interreligious dialogue and cooperation. In particular it emphasised the defusing of tensions between the Western and Islamic worlds so new partnerships could be established promoting global understanding.

The first forum was held in Madrid in 2008, attended by over 900 participants from 78 countries. Since then there have been forums in Turkey and Brazil.

FALSE GOSPELS

It is claimed that a New World Order and a 'planetary consciousness' is developing. A number of trends support this view, not least the growing call for:

* Global disarmament
* One world government (global governance)
* A return to paganism
* Environmental extremism
* Socialism and communism
* Religious persecution in the name of 'tolerance' and combating 'hate'.

To assure its success, the New World Order requires a One World Religion and its proponents are already at work. Globalist theologian Lloyd Geering in his book 'The World to Come,' says:

If the global society emerges, it will require humanity to develop a new consciousness and a new form of spirituality . . . If the human species is not to self-destruct it must develop into a global society which will find cohesion in what may be called a global human culture. The challenges which lie ahead cannot be overcome by any one person or group working on their own but only by the human species working as a whole

In 1996 the United Nations published a 420 page report: 'Our Global Neighbourhood', which outlined a plan for global governance. By 1996 the term 'global governance' had replaced 'New World Order' in such communications. The thesis advocated not just global governance, but also One World Religion. Vera Alder, a teacher in esoteric knowledge says in her book 'When Humanity Comes':

There is actually a Plan and a Purpose behind all creation. World unity is the goal towards which evolution is moving. The world plan includes: A World Organization, a World Economy, a World Religion.

As radical liberal theologians were declaring the death of God and the Bible in the 60s, others were announcing the return of the gods and goddesses of ancient Greece and Rome. Today's Postmodern theologians declare that religion is not in decline, but simply in a process of reformation. As in ancient Rome social and religious forces are working together. Western capitalism is partnering with Eastern meditation.

With the rebirth of pagan goddess worship and Christianity in decline, or at least being re-imagined, I believe that we're set to see the great apostasy (Christians turning away from the true faith) spoken about by Jesus (Matt 24:12) and the coming political, economic and religious system under the control of the Antichrist (Rev 13).

How do we share the Gospel?

As the global culture becomes more pagan and Western culture shakes off its Christian heritage, Christians are marginalised and they lose confidence and retreat from the public square. As a result, some are now asking the question: How should we share the Gospel in a Postmodern, post-Christian, post-national and increasingly global situation?

In answering this question some are proposing that we change the Gospel message and embrace a new unifying religion for the sake of the planet. Many see the extreme liberal wing of the Postmodern Emergent Church as the precursor to the 'religion of tolerance' that will cause many within the Church to fall away and ultimately to embrace the One World Religion under the Antichrist.

Mick Bickle (International House of Prayer: Kansas) in his 'Omega Course' notes, says:

The rise of false christs and prophets will help establish alliances between all the false religions which include the occult, New Age, Muslims, Hindus, Buddhists and liberal 'Christianity' with a commitment to moral tolerance that paves the way for a one world religion.

The Bible is clear concerning the direction the world will take. Whilst in this chapter I will focus on the religious system, we need to understand that it is developing in tandem with the political and economic systems and all three will ultimately emerge as one entity.

The essence of the emerging One World Religion (the New Spirituality) is that 'all roads lead to God,' and that all so-called gods are equally valid, each having a part of the truth. Religious pluralism and syncretism (merging of religious practices) and Universalism (everybody is saved in the end) are its tenets.

Also implicit is the notion that One World Religion provides an answer to religious conflict, whilst supporting globalization, the new world order and our efforts to save the planet. Whilst Postmodernism shuns meta-narratives (over-arching worldviews), intellectual elites, mystics, the liberal Emerging Church, New Agers and neo-pagans are eagerly pursuing a coherent worldview to save the planet.

Driving the agenda

In his book 'One or Two', Peter Jones says:

. . . thousands of progressives in academics, the media and politics, along with the liberal church leaders are joining to produce a pagan cosmology to repair our deconstructed world.

Religious evolution, they claim, is coming of age. The so-called New Spirituality is now very much on the agenda. It's driven by Postmodern, liberal, religious and ideologically driven individuals and groups within the intelligentsia, who consider themselves to be the ruling elite, progressive, open-minded and intellectually and spiritually enlightened.

For the One World Religion to become a reality, religion has to become an essential part of life for everyone and whilst Christianity is being ousted, false religions have taken a hold and are now being accepted by people who would not previously have professed to be religious in any way. It's now trendy to be 'spiritual.' More and more people say: 'I'm not religious, but I am spiritual'.

According to Peter Jones, in his book 'One or Two,' Western culture, has been hijacked by a spiritual ideology that he calls Neo-Paganism (new-paganism) or as we would say New Spirituality. Whilst horoscopes, fortune-tellers, Halloween and Harry Potter are the closest most people get to paganism, John Frame in the foreword to the book 'On Global Wizardry,' reminds us of a sobering truth:

Few realise that this new paganism is an historical and worldwide movement of enormous cultural power, one that has sought for centuries, and still seeks, to dominate our world.

In essence, the emerging One World Religion/New Spirituality is a reappearance and networking of ancient forms of spirituality, including aspects of the following:

The mystery religions; esoteric (hidden and mysterious); the occult (hidden); religious paganism (local religions); pre-Christian goddess worship; shamanism (ways of communicating with the spirit world); animism (non-living objects have a life force); witchcraft; Eastern mysticism (Buddhism, Hinduism, yoga and so on); ancient Gnosticism (secret knowledge); Desert Fathers; Catholic mysticism; New Age practices; religious syncretism (merging of religious practices); secret societies and inter-spirituality (interfaith).

The New Spirituality movement is an alignment of all that's opposed to the will of God. It's vehemently opposed to the Christian faith. Frame, in the foreword to the book 'On Global Wizardry,' says:

These movements are parallel to one another, even congruent. So they form a single movement in effect. They work together, drawing on one another for support and inspiration, affirming one another, while they unite in opposing biblical Christianity. The resulting movement is, then, a work of Satan seeking to confront Christianity head-on. Whilst this paganism is imprecise it is in effect the sum of every unrelated non-Christian religion.

According to Dr Peter Jones in his book 'Spirit Wars':

It is vitally important to see beyond the external diversity and subtle distinctions to the inner coherence of paganism which is known as Monism.

In essence Monism claims that the universe is a mass of undifferentiated, related energy. God is not distinct and outside the universe, he is the universe. The Creator/creature distinction has been eradicated.

The New Spirituality mixture of beliefs and practices, it should be said, not only impacts the liberal Emerging Church, but every sphere of society - government, education, health-care, media, business, ecology, religion, law-making, globalisation, interfaith religion, psychology, sociology, science, arts, entertainment, sports etc.

Peter Jones in his book 'Spirit Wars,' says:

Gone is the skeptical liberal re-interpretation of the Gospel in terms of social involvement or Marxist theory. New liberalism has discovered a spirituality that will save the planet and fulfill the goals of an aspiring humanity. The liberal vision of an inclusive egalitarian culture of the future - 'America as it was meant to be!' - conceives of a new world where the distinctions between the sexes, between right and wrong, between true and false are blurred, where Satan is but the creation of wild-eyed fundamentalists, where tolerance for all - except orthodox Christianity - is the highest good.

This is not dry theory. The new liberals teach our children in schools and universities, influence the media by claiming to speak for the Church and for the best interest of the planet, and take positions of political leadership in our very religious country. And now they have spiritual power to back them up.

Western society generally is rejecting Judaeo-Christian values and worldview. Just as secular humanism has questioned the presuppositions of orthodox evangelical Christianity so does neo-paganism. Some would argue that neo-paganism has largely replaced secular humanism as the dominant ideology of our time. In any event Judaeo-Christian values are caught in a pincer movement and increasingly excluded from the public square.

Whilst the liberal Emerging Church, the resurgence of ancient forms of mystical spirituality/religious paganism and the shift from Modernism to Postmodernism are distinct and separate entities which have enjoyed parallel development for a number of years (decades in fact), there has nevertheless been a great deal of cross fertilisation and merging of ideas and practices.

No one speaks for the emerging One world Religion/New Spirituality movement as a whole and no one speaks for anyone else within the movement. It can mean many different things to those within it and there's no headquarters you can call up to request information.

New Spirituality: Neo-Paganism

There are a number of core beliefs in the emerging One World Religion/New Spirituality, which the Postmodern worldview supports:

*   It's anti-Christian
*   It's mystical; experience is everything, just as with Postmodernism
*   It believes that each of the world's religious traditions shares a single universal truth. It believes that the divine has manifested itself through many deities in different places and at different times. So no one deity can express the totality of the divine
*   It holds to the view that all religions are attempts by the Occult Brotherhood to help humanity in evolving to greater perfection
*   It aims to create a spirituality that is inclusive and pluralistic (all religions are valid)
*   It draws on both Eastern and Western mystical, spiritual and supernatural traditions and infuses them with influences from self help, motivational psychology and holistic health – Reiki healing (occult or ghost energy), yoga (based on the Chakra system drawing on Kundalini or Serpent Power).
*   It's both Pantheistic and Panentheistic - the divine is present in nature and in each one of us. The divine is everywhere and in everyone. Indeed, everything and everyone is divine
*   The divine is both male and female - the god and goddess, although the divine is beyond limitations of gender
*   The Pagan Ethic (also called the Wiccan Rede) is followed: 'If it

harm none, do what you will.' This means a pagan cannot cause harm to anyone or anything, including themselves or nature. Other than that they're free to do anything

The change to the Postmodern worldview around the middle of the last century presented the New Age pagans with a wonderful opportunity. Spiritual darkness is increasing and becoming more sophisticated and the strongholds that the enemy is using are deeply rooted in the actions of past generations. As Christians we do not fully understand the spiritual dimension as well as we ought. George Otis Jnr in his book 'The Twilight Labyrinth,' says:

Strongholds are born whenever individuals, societies and cultures welcome evil powers into their midst . . . The enemy gains dominion over human systems - political, economic and religious . . .Despite the countervailing influence of Judaeo-Christian values, dark powers have managed to secure a foothold in Europe and America.

In just one generation, Judaeo-Christian Western culture has become an incubator of revived paganism. Peter Jones in his book 'One or Two,' says:

Neo-pagans are the darling of a variety of movements. They lead the way in the 'green' movement, in systems of wealth distribution, in planetary programmes for social justice, in solutions to supposedly man-made global warming, in interfaith conferences, in the normalisation of all sexual expressions and in the promotion of globalist theories through the United Nations (UN).

The New Spirituality is changing the spiritual landscape of the Western world and society is being conditioned to accept this false spirituality that rejects the Gospel. In his book 'Spirit Wars,' he says:

This revolution penetrates every home and soul, redefining sexuality, spirituality, God, religion and revelation. The new world order turns everything we have known on its head - good becomes evil, homosexuality the preferred sexual expression and the traditional family a minority structure.

Today, a programme of mystical spirituality, social justice, inter-faith and world peace is proposed as the answer to all man's ills. Many with immense power and wealth, empowered by the New Spirituality, believe that an earthly, planetary Utopia is just around the corner.

Involvement of the liberal Emerging Church

So why would the liberal Emerging Church want to be identified with the New Spirituality? And why would the New Spirituality be ready to accept the liberal Emerging Church within its fold, bearing in mind it's opposed to biblical Christianity?

The liberal Emerging Church has bought into the Postmodern way of relating to the world. Because it's also willing to compromise and change the Gospel - both its message and practice – to suit the Postmodern culture, it finds a warm welcome at the emerging New Spirituality's 'conversation.'

Whilst the liberal Emerging Church likes to think of itself as a key spiritual player in the New Spirituality, in reality it's only a small fish in a large pagan pond. The New Spirituality is set on becoming a global religion embracing all religions and none, under the Antichrist. Every religion and ideology will serve Lucifer at the end of the age. The goal of the emerging One World Religion/New Spirituality fits perfectly with biblical prophecy:

Men worshiped the dragon because he had given authority to the beast, and they also worshiped the beast and asked, 'Who is like the beast? Who can make war against him?' . . . He opened his mouth to blaspheme God, and to slander his name . . . All inhabitants of the earth will worship the beast - all whose names have not been written in the book of life belonging to the Lamb that was slain from the creation of the world (Rev 13:4-8 part).

Jesus warns us in Mathews Gospel that many false prophets will rise and lead many astray at the end of the age:

At that time many will turn away from the faith and will betray and hate each other, and many false prophets will appear and deceive many people. Because of the increase of wickedness, the love of most will grow cold, but he who stands firm to the end will be saved (Matt 24:10-14).

Whilst the liberal Emerging Church prides itself on its pioneering spirit, in reality, the truth is that it has simply swallowed the enemy's deception. It has left the one true Church and embraced a new humanistic and pagan agenda. It has exchanged the truth for a lie.

For example, Brian McLaren the acknowledged leader of the Emerging Church is associated with futuristic groups that worship the earth and reject its Creator. He was a featured speaker at the Walter H. Capps Centre, a group devoted to the challenges of pluralism.

Other featured speakers included: Elaine Pagels (a Gnostic); Mary Tucker (a Buddhist); Starhawk (a witch); Peter Russell (a New Age guru); and Diana Eck (lesbian Professor of Religion at Harvard). When given the opportunity to share the Gospel this is what he said:

* The Church's difficulties are self-imposed; we have the gospel all wrong and need to modify it
* We should avoid mentioning sin, the cross or personal salvation, since these terms don't sit well today
* Christians should drop their concern with personal survival in the afterlife, to focus on helping the poor and saving the environment

Whilst the liberal Emerging Church presents the biggest challenge to biblical evangelical Christianity for decades, and we shouldn't underestimate the harm it can do, nevertheless it reflects a somewhat pathetic image if you compare it to the vibrant Church of Jesus Christ which down through the ages has and will continue to robustly defend the truth of the Gospel – refusing to embrace the ideas and practices of either Postmodernism or the New Spirituality.

FOUNDATION OF AMERICA

Our history textbooks tell us that the men, women and children, who travelled across the Atlantic to the New World from England and the Netherlands to escape persecution by the church in 1620, were staunch Puritan Christians.

They landed at Plymouth and settled on the East coast of America and worked the land in order to survive. They built their schools and cities founded on Christian principles revealed in the Bible. From this beginning it is said that their descendants went on to found the United States of America as a Christian nation, 'the land of the free.' At least that's what the Patriotic wing of the Christian Right in America would have us believe.

Esoteric beginnings

Unfortunately, however, that's not the full picture and historians and researchers suggest that there's a different story to tell. A story with two movements developing in parallel, each with its own version of reality. That of the Puritans on the one hand and on the other a powerful, mysterious, occult, luciferian and secretive group.

They deem that very early on in the populating of the New World, members of secret societies also arrived on America's shores from Europe with a completely different agenda. These were largely children of the Enlightenment, Rosicrucians and Freemasons who arrived with a revolutionary spirit and an 'ancient hope' of establishing a new world order - some would even suggest to do with rebuilding of the lost empire of Atlantis.

Two sided coin

There can be no doubt that much of America's national heritage was Christian, but just as a coin has two sides, America's heritage has a second side. Only when you consider the occult heritage set in place through the American Revolution by the Founding Fathers in 1776, over 150 years after the original pilgrims landed, can you begin to understand some of the actions of its leaders over the centuries.

Hidden agenda

We will explore the agenda of the Founding Fathers, many of whom were members of secret societies, later in this article. The agenda of the secret societies over the past 230 years has been kept hidden by means of a deliberate subterfuge and a strategy of limiting knowledge to lower degree members, clothing their ideas wherever possible in a garment of Christian phraseology and using legitimate power structures (presidents, government officials, oligarchs, bankers etc.) to implement their plans. Only the Founding Fathers, the very highest illuminates (e.g. 33rd degree Masons) within the secret societies, high level neo-pagans and New Agers would be able to provide answers, I would suggest, to the following questions.

Important questions

If America was founded as a Christian nation by the Founding Fathers, why are many of its symbols, buildings, and monuments based on Pagan traditions? Why is Washington D.C. build on the 77th Meridian and why are the Revolutionary War cities on the east coast (Washington, Baltimore, Philadelphia, New York and Boston) built in perfect alignment with each other and, more to the point, with Stonehenge?

Why is Washington DC, as some believe, laid out 'according to the stars,' i.e., in the astrological shapes of certain planets and stars so revered by occultists? Why did the Masonic Founding Fathers perform 'Corn, Wine, and Oil' ceremonies at cornerstone laying and at the dedication of finished structures? Why is the Great Seal of America a Masonic emblem and how did it end up on the back of the dollar bill? More to the point, if America was founded as a Christian nation, where are the images of Jesus Christ? Why are so many former presidents both Masons and members of other secret societies like Skull and Bones?

Influence

Which of these two founding movements has had the greatest influence on American society, is open to debate. What is undeniable however is that whereas orthodox Christianity is increasingly marginalised in America today, there are growing numbers of pseudo-Christians, Emergents, New Agers, members of secret societies and neo-pagans who believe that a new pantheistic spirituality is required, an aspect of which will render the old world order of sovereign states and Judaeo-Christian values obsolete. They are more than ready to embrace a new world order based on occult principles.

Exposed

Today, in order to combat this luciferian agenda the Holy Spirit's leading researchers to uncover the hidden layers of America's beginnings and in so doing is exposing a trail of esoteric activity. America's position and influence on the world stage demands clarity and honesty around such issues.

Founding Fathers (Thomas Paine)

In exploring these issues we will begin our journey by considering the Revolutionary era and look at the beliefs and practices of the Founding Fathers. The American Revolution begins with Thomas Paine. Paine was an English author, radical, inventor, intellectual and revolutionary.

He met Benjamin Franklin in London who suggested he emigrate to British colonial America, and gave him a letter of recommendation. He duly emigrated in 1774 in time to participate in the American Revolution. He advocated America's independence from the Kingdom of Great Britain and wrote a pamphlet entitled 'Common Sense' which influenced Thomas Jefferson's writing of the Declaration of Independence.

The pamphlet appeared in January 1776, after the Revolution had started. It was passed around and contributed significantly to spreading the idea of republicanism, bolstering enthusiasm for separation from Britain, and encouraging recruitment for the Continental Army.

In late 1776 Paine published 'The Crisis' series to inspire the Americans in their battles against the British army. John Adams said, 'Without the pen of Pain, the sword of Washington would have been wielded in vain.' A quote on Paine's tombstone says:

History is to ascribe the American Revolution to Thomas Paine

Paine lived in France for most of the 1790s, becoming deeply involved in the French Revolution. He wrote the 'Rights of Man' (1791) in defense of the French Revolution and The 'Age of Reason' (1793-4) in which he advocated deism, promoted reason and free-thinking, argued against institutionalised religion and Christian doctrines.

So was Thomas Paine a Bible-believing Christian? We should let him speak for himself. He described himself as a deist saying:

How different is [Christianity] to the pure and simple profession of Deism! The true Deist has but one Deity, and his religion consists in contemplating the power, wisdom, and benignity of the Deity in his works, and in endeavoring to imitate him in everything moral, scientifical, and mechanical.

In the 'Age of Reason' he says:

I believe in one God, and no more; and I hope for happiness beyond this life. I believe in the equality of man; and I believe that religious duties consist in doing justice, loving mercy, and endeavoring to make our fellow-creatures happy.

I do not believe in the creed professed by the Jewish church, by the Roman church, by the Greek church, by the Turkish church, by the Protestant church nor by any church that I know of. My own mind is my own church. All national institutions of churches, whether Jewish, Christian or Turkish, appear to me no other than human inventions, set up to terrify and enslave mankind, and monopolize power and profit.

About the Bible, he said:

When I see throughout the greater part of this book (the Bible) scarcely anything but a history of the grossest vices and a collection of the most paltry and contemptible tales, I cannot dishonour my Creator by calling it by his name.

What is it the Bible teaches us? - rapine, cruelty, and murder. What is it the Testament teaches us? - to believe that the Almighty committed debauchery with a woman engaged to be married, and the belief of this debauchery is called faith.

It is the fable of Jesus Christ, as told in the New Testament, and the wild and visionary doctrine raised thereon, against which I contend. The story, taking it as it is told, is blasphemously obscene.

It is clear that Thomas Paine was not a Bible-believing Christian! He was no more than a product of the Enlightenment and a rationalist, and consequently there is no evidence that his desire was to found America as a Christian nation. At the very best he was simply a believer in good works.

Thomas Jefferson

Jefferson is commonly known as someone who considered Jesus to be a fine teacher of morality, but he certainly did not believe in the authority of the Bible. He wrote extensively about separating the 'true' sayings of Jesus to the things he believed had been added to the accounts in the Gospels. His 'Jefferson Bible' specifically removed the virgin birth, the miracles of Jesus, the resurrection and the ascension, plus the entire book of Revelation. In a letter about the Bible written in 1820 he said:

I find many passages of fine imagination, correct morality, and of the most lovely benevolence; and others, again, of so much ignorance, so much absurdity, so much untruth, charlatanism and imposture.

Jefferson rejected the idea of immaterial beings and considered the idea of an immaterial Creator a heresy introduced into Christianity. Jefferson is often seen as an icon of American democracy, liberty and independence. Abraham Lincoln once said that he was 'the most distinguished politician in our history'.

Benjamin Franklin

Benjamin Franklin is well known for his discovery of electricity. He was not only a scientist but also a patriot, a Freemason and a significant influence in the founding of America. Sir Walter Isaacs said of him:

The most accomplished American of his age and the most influential in inventing the type of society America would become.

In fact he was the only Founding Father who signed all the documents for the establishment of the United States (i.e. the Declaration of Independence; the US Constitution and the Treaty of Paris (which brought the war with the UK to an end).

However, as a high-ranking Freemason in America, the UK and in France, his over-riding religious belief was that salvation was based on good works. Contrary to genuine Christian belief, he once said:

Original sin is as ridiculous as imputed righteousness.

Indeed, his religious views were strongly shaped by the Enlightenment thinkers of the 18th century. He doubted the divinity of Jesus, as he wrote in a letter to Ezra Styles, president of Yale University:

It (the divinity of Jesus) is a question I do not dogmatise upon, having never studied it, and I think it needless to busy myself with it now.

His UK connection with Freemasonry was as a member of Francis Dashwood's Hellfire Club, where satanic rites and orgies were undertaken. In 1998 the Sunday Times reported:

Workmen have dug up the remains of 10 bodies hidden beneath the former London home of Benjamin Franklin, the Founding Father of American Independence. The remains of 4 adults and 6 children were discovered during the restoration of Benjamin Franklin's home at 36 Craven Street.

Some investigators suspected that the remains, which dated from his time of residence in the property, could point to human sacrifices carried out in the Hellfire Club.

John Adams

Adams, America's second president and first vice-president worked with Thomas Jefferson to draft the Declaration of Independence. Whilst there is no proof that he was a member of any secret society, he was, however, a Unitarian. His basic belief therefore was that God is unknowable; to say that Jesus Christ is God and that he came to make God known would be considered blasphemy.

Adams is credited with laying down the principles on which the United States would be built. In relation to these foundational principles, Adams said:

These are what are called revolution principles. They are the principles of Aristotle and Plato . . . the principles of nature and eternal reason.

He referred to the general principles on which the Founding Fathers achieved independence as the 'general principles of Christianity,' yet he remarked that he could find a multitude of quotations from Rousseau and Voltaire in favour of these principles. We know, however, that both these men had strong anti-Christian views. For example, Voltaire said:

It took twelve ignorant fishermen to establish Christianity. I will show the world how one Frenchman can destroy it.

When Adams and those who influenced him spoke of religious freedom their vision was to be free of Christianity. Adams gleaned many of his beliefs from an ancient Indian writing, the Shasta. In a letter to Thomas Jefferson he wrote:

Where is to be found theology more orthodox, or philosophy more profound, than in the introduction to the Shasta?

Hardly the comment of a committed Christian!

The Treaty of Tripoli

This treaty was signed by Adams in 1796. Article 11, which was drafted by George Washington, and unanimously agreed by the Senate, states categorically:

The Government of the United States is not in any sense founded on the Christian religion.

Historian Bird Wilson stated in a sermon in 1831 that the founders of the US were nearly all infidels. God was not overlooked; he was deliberately voted out of the Constitution.

George Washington

Washington, after whom the capital city of the US is named, is known as the 'Father of America.' The Treaty of Tripoli was drafted towards the end of his term of office as president, and confirmed during Adams' presidency.

Washington's Christian faith is questionable. He had a habit of attending church regularly but he avoided communion services. Pastor James Abercrombie remarked that Washington was a deist. Washington wrote to the Delaware Indians encouraging them to learn the religion of Jesus Christ, yet his letters to Lafayette give the impression that he went through the motions of Christianity without having a personal belief or faith.

Just hours before his death, Washington was baptised by a Jesuit priest into the Roman Catholic religion. His sympathies were with the Catholics long before that, indicated by his refusal to burn effigies of the Pope.

The Stars and Stripes

It is very possible that the design for the American flag came from Laurentius Ricci, the leader of the Jesuit order, who influenced George Washington. Tupper Saussy says that Ricci stated:

Americans would be fighting under the private flag of an international mercantile corporation controlled by Jesuits.

In the course of time, the flag developed into the familiar Stars and Stripes we know today.

Religious liberty

George Washington is known to have said that the establishment of civil and religious liberty was the motive that induced him into the field (of war and politics). But by religious liberty he meant a licence for all religions to have equal place in America. This view concurs with the Freemasonry universalist view, that all religions must be tolerated with no weight given to any particular one.

It may be that there was a hidden agenda behind Washington's statements, bearing in mind his Roman Catholic leanings. Back in the 17th century when James II was king of England, James called for all religious restraints to be removed. As a Roman Catholic himself, his motivation was to allow tolerance for Roman Catholics, couching it in perceived liberty for all faiths. James was deposed, Roman Catholicism suppressed and a Protestant monarch took the throne.

In America, however, the Constitution was worded to appear to promote freedom for all religions yet the primary motivation was to protect Roman Catholics and keep Jesuits safe.

Is America a Christian nation?

Whilst the Pilgrim Fathers had a genuine Christian faith, the Founding Fathers we've looked at in this article clearly had not. Their world view was shaped by the Enlightenment, Freemasonry and Eastern spirituality. I believe it's important to be aware of this, and to recognise the effects their influence has had, and still has, on America today.

The Presidents of the United States

There are many web sites which document the ancestry of the US Presidents. All but one (Martin van Beuren) can trace their ancestry to the Plantagenet rulers of England, post 1066. Most can trace it to one particular king of England in the Angevin part of the Plantagenet dynasty – King John (Lackland), who was made to sign the Magna Carta in 1215. It is remarkable that a 'free' vote should produce presidents with a common blood line and begs the question, is it coincidence, or were they chosen? If so, by whom and why?

The answer may lie in the religion and philosophy in the foundation of the United States. We have expanded on the Founding Fathers, but it's important to note that they were heavily influenced by Freemasonry. In January 2007, the 110th Congress passed House Resolution 33, which recognised:

The thousands of Freemasons in every State in the Nation . . . Whereas the Founding Fathers of this great Nation and signers of the Constitution, most of whom were Freemasons, provided a well-rounded basis for developing themselves and others into valuable citizens of the United States.

Satanic roots of Freemasonry

American Freemasonry can be traced back to England during the lifetime of Sir Francis Bacon (1561-1626). He is considered to be the first grand master of modern Masonry. He was a close associate of Dr John Dee, Elizabeth I's court astrologer. Dee was a sorcerer who summoned demonic spirits to obtain secret knowledge, an art he acquired from his involvement with the Rosicrucians. In order to obtain secret knowledge, Rosicrucians consulted demons. It is known that Bacon gained his inspiration from his spirit guide, known as Pallas Athena. Bacon succeeded Dee as the leader of the Rosicrucians, and Bacon amalgamated many of their secrets into the system of Freemasonry.

Rosicrucians

It was the desire to obtain knowledge that drove Rosicrucians, like the Gnostics before them, to worship Lucifer. The secret societies consider Lucifer to be the angel of light, who encouraged mankind to eat from the Tree of Knowledge of Good and Evil so their eyes would be opened and they would be as gods.

In this they concur with the corrupted creation myths of ancient civilisations other than the Israelites. This is the inner doctrine of Rosicrucianism, Freemasonry and all the secret societies. It became known that this was the case when the writings of key Freemasons and occultists such as Albert Pike, Mackey, Eliphas Levi and Madame Blavatsky were published in the 19th century.

Knights Templar

The Knights Templar, another secret society, fled to Scotland in the 14th century when they were persecuted in Europe. The red cross of the Templars is likely to be the point of origin for the rose cross of Rosicrucianism. When the Scottish Jacobite rebellions broke out in the early 1700s, many Scottish Freemasons and Rosicrucians fled to America, taking their occultism with them. One of their power centres was the Fredericksburg Lodge No 4, whose members included George Washington, James Monroe and eight of the Revolutionary War generals.

Washington DC

Carving their doctrines in stone, seen in Rosslyn Chapel in Edinburgh, was a practice which was continued by the Freemasons with the building of Washington DC. There are countless images of gods and goddesses there, along with zodiacs, the Washington Monument obelisk, reflecting pools, myriads of pagan images and a pentagram street layout. Any reference to Jesus Christ or Christianity is absent.

In light of all this, with such demonic roots, it does not seem so fanciful to believe that US presidents are appointed not so much by the will of man but of Satan. The land they govern, Francis Bacon's 'New Atlantis', could also be called the 'Land of the Rosicrucians.' Their demonic influence from Bacon's time onwards has caused America to be what she is. Because Rosicrucians and Freemasons happily mingle Christianity with paganism they can give the appearance of being 'Christian' while equally exalting the teachings of Plato and other philosophers. They see the ancient gods as examples of virtue and justice as much as they give lip service to the moral teachings of Jesus.

WASHINGTON DC

Washington DC was founded by George Washington, Thomas Jefferson and others, and it is a city full of arcane symbols and mythological characters. A close examination of the layout reveals that Freemasonry symbolism is intrinsic in the design. As we've mentioned, the Founding Fathers were either proven Freemasons or heavily influenced by them and this is evident in the city they conceived.

The symbols they used have two meanings; the esoteric intended for the few who can read and understand them, and the exoteric for the many who appreciate them only at a more superficial level.

The cornerstone of the US Capitol Building was laid by George Washington in 1793 in a typical Freemasonry ceremony where corn, wine and oil were used. In antiquity corn symbolises plenty, wine symbolises refreshment and oil symbolises joy; there are however different levels of interpretation for these symbols in Freemasonry. Senator Thurman, a 33rd degree Mason was involved in the 200th anniversary celebrations of the laying of the foundation stone.

Baal
Baal, the antithesis of the God of the Bible, is depicted in Phoenician art as a bearded figure very similar to some of the images seen in Washington DC. Some even have corn in their hair. Corn, wine

and oil were used in Baal worship in Canaan. Baal, the god of corn as well as the sun and the weather, dies and is resurrected (or awakened) in some legends.

In Washington DC there is a statue of a bearded giant rising out of the ground, called 'The Awakening.' Another landmark in the city, the monument or obelisk, is a symbol of resurrection in Freemasonry, referred to as the Baal shaft. This gives us an indication that Baal, not the God of the Bible, is venerated in Washington DC.

The god of Freemasonry

Freemasons at the higher levels worship a god with a name that amalgamates three words for god in ancient religions (Jehovah, Baal and Osiris) – Jebelon. The attributes of this god are summed up as 'The Great Architect of the Universe.' This god is the antithesis of the one true God.

Sirius, the Dog Star

Sirius is called the dog-star after Anubis, the ancient Egyptian dog-shaped god who protected the mysteries and the gates of death (hell, hades or the underworld). It's also believed to be the all-seeing eye, or Horus, the child of the goddess Isis, who was born at the magical moment when the Nile floods, coinciding with Sirius rising in the sky.

The all-seeing eye can be seen on the US dollar bill where the capstone should be, illuminated not by the sun but by Sirius. In Freemasonry, the Blazing Star (Horus, Sirius or all-seeing eye) is the offspring of the male sun and female moon.

In his book, 'Founding Fathers; Secret Societies,' Hieronomus explains that in ancient mystery cults, at first the sun is said to be a god; priests at the second level learn that spirit and energy flow through the sun; but at the third level, which only selected priests would know about, they recognise Sirius the Dog Star, not the sun, as the most important star. It was considered the brightest star in the heavens, brighter than the sun, yet the most evil star in the sky.

The Great Pyramid (as well as other ancient artifacts) was aligned with Sirius. When this star began its ascendancy, the Nile was in drought and weak (July). The Declaration of Independence was signed when the sun was aligned with Sirius (July 1776), and the cornerstone of the Monument was laid when Sirius would have been rising to the East. The Monument, an Egyptian-style obelisk aligns with the Masonic Temple built some years later. The original plan was to align it due south of the White House, but the location would not support its weight.

The Washington Monument

The construction work began in July 1848 and took 30 years to complete. The final design, by George Marsh, the father of the environmentalist movement, was much simpler than the original plan, and shorter. Whilst most obelisks are made from one block of stone, this one is made of many. It has a pyramid at the top of the 13 levels, like the one on the dollar bill. In the vicinity there is a buried miniature replica of the obelisk, but it lacks a capstone, as does the one on the dollar bill.

It is thought that the missing capstone on the pyramid on the US dollar bill has been replaced with the all-seeing eye and the illumination around the eye is not the sun but Sirius. The return of the capstone signifies the return of the Freemasonry cosmic Christ.

Pentagrams

The symbol for Sirius is a five-pointed star. One may be found beneath the altar in every Masonic Lodge, in the centre of the building. The ancient Gnostic term for Sirius is 'Blazing Star,' and it is referred to as such by Albert Pike. Another notable Freemason,

Alistair Crowley belonged to a secret society named the 'Order of the Silver Star.'

Democracy and the 'American Dream'

The Founding Fathers founded America inspired by the writings of Plato. Manly P Hall, writing at the beginning of the 20th century, was convinced that America had a secret destiny. According to him, the secret societies were secretly committed to world democracy, which flew in the face of monarchs who believed in the divine right of kings. They therefore had to keep it secret as it was seen as treason.

Democracy contains the occult promise of a fair world for all to share. Freemason F D Roosevelt, for example, believed he was creating a new democracy and liberty out of the ashes of the depression following the war. Other more recent presidents, such as G W Bush, were committed to the same dream. But to further the dream, the true beliefs and process need to be kept hidden or secret, hence the elaborate initiation ceremonies of secret societies.

While many American leaders have upheld Christian ideals, they may have done so to protect their occult philosophies.

Rosicrucian influence

We know that Francis Bacon was heavily influenced by Rosicrucianism, and there are many symbols associated with it in the Capitol building and elsewhere in the city of Washington DC. Pallas Athena, Bacon's goddess inspiration, can be seen depicted in many sculptures in the city, as well as Bacon's effigy in the Library of Congress. The city is located on the 77th Meridian, considered sacred by esoterics.

Bacon's book reveals that the New Atlantis was a hope, not a dream and the ancient city of Atlantis was not just a myth or legend. Indeed, Plato cited Solen as the source of his belief in Atlantis and Solen in turn cited the priests of ancient Egypt as his source. All these people believed that all knowledge and god-like powers hidden within secret societies originated there. It would appear that the Knights Templar brought back the secret knowledge from the Middle East, and Bacon and others took them to the New World.

Hermeticism

The mysticism of ancient Egypt which stretched back to about 3000BC mingled with Greek traditions such as Pythagoreanism and Platonism in the time of Alexander the Great. The Egyptian god of wisdom, Thoth the Thrice-Great (or Trismegistus in Latin) was identified with the Greek god of writing and communication, Hermes, producing a compound figure known as Hermes Trimegistus.

Writings about magic and mysticism were attributed to him and he became accepted as a legendary godlike person from pre-biblical times with prehistoric wisdom. He became the legendary founder of architecture and masonry, for example.

In reality, most of the works attributed to Hermes Trimegistus originated in Alexandria in the first few centuries AD. The body of work became known as the Corpus Hermeticum, and dealt with all manner of topics including magic, spells, Gnostic religion, Pythagorean mathematics, Platonic philosophy and alchemy.

The works were preserved by Islamic scholars and rediscovered in 1453 by an Italian scholar who came across a manuscript. The contents seemed to be a direct line to prehistoric wisdom and became known as Hermetic philosophy or Hermeticism. It was a major influence in the development of secret societies.

The Hermetic maxim, 'as above, so below,' is seen today in reflecting pools and esoteric art in Washington DC. The Pythagorean triangle when reflected makes the six pointed star or hexagram. From the belief that what is in the heavens has to reflect, at a point in time, what is on the earth, buildings were constructed to align with the stars and thus with the ruling spirits which guide the stars.

The street plan of Washington DC

Whilst opinions differ, some say there are distinct Masonic symbols in the layout of the city of Washington DC. Certainly the first plan, designed by Freemason Pierre Charles L'Enfant varies only a little from the modern city layout, despite others being involved after he was fired from the planning.

Pythagoreanism

Freemason David Ovason says that the real mystery in the city is in Federal Triangle. There is a triangle of stars surrounding Virgo shaped like a Pythagorean triangle, and which has significance in Pythagorean theory.

The White House, Capitol Building and Washington monument are in a triangle replicating the three stars above which surround Virgo. This was intentional ('as above, so below') to draw on the spiritual energies associated with Virgo.

It could be so designed to enable Virgo to bring forth the divine child. The cosmic child is symbolised by one side of the triangle; the male and female are the other two sides. The hypotenuse of the triangle is Pennsylvania Avenue. Symbolically, this then becomes the spiritual centre of Washington DC, symbolising the divine offspring of the divine trinity.

Alchemy and the cosmic Christ

The divine child, or cosmic Christ, is the messiah esoterics are looking for, the result of the joining of cosmic masculine and feminine forces. Versions of the way this can be achieved are found in esoteric writings and beliefs of all kinds, including alchemy (the Arabic term for chemistry). The goal of alchemy is divine chemistry, i.e. the transformation of the lower self to the higher self.

Alchemy is based on the view that man, as a result of the loss of his original Adamic state, is divided within himself. He regains his integral nature only when the two powers . . . are again reconciled with one another. (from 'the (Al)Chemical Marriage of Christian Rosenkreutz' quoted in a web site article).

In Washington DC examples abound of male images with corresponding female images, and a perfected child between them. The latter is often the figure of a prominent Freemason.

One representation is the Boy Scout Memorial, where the Boy Scout stands in the place of the divine offspring. Daniel Carter Beard, a Freemason, started the Boy Scout movement in America. Likewise, the Masonic Temple has a male figure one side and a female figure on the other. In this case, the pediment between them has the goddess Liberty at its centre; Liberty represents the perfected child.

SURVEILLANCE SOCIETY

We have entered an era of shadow government - powerful agencies collect data on every one of us. They observe our private lives and record the information on computer files. Government authorities, national security agencies and businesses that market and sell consumer products know far more about us than even our close friends and family.

They know where we live, the type of property we live in, our mortgage details, our medical history, our educational background, employment status, vehicle ownership, driving record, criminal record, credit rating, tax records, what we watch on pay-TV, our financial assets and in some cases our fingerprint and DNA information. They track our movements and monitor every telephone call, fax, Internet search and email transmission we make.

Big Brother already knows and it's virtually impossible to retrieve your privacy.

Justification

They justify this invasion of privacy by reminding us of the threat posed by international terrorists, organised crime, illegal immigrants, welfare cheats and tax evaders. Tragically the average individual is blissfully unaware. High-tech surveillance methods are stealing one of our most basic human rights - the right to privacy and the right to be left alone.

1984 and George Orwell?

CCTV today is far more invasive than any of us could have imagined when it first came into use. Although the cameras have displaced violent crime rather than suppressed it, there were 4.2 million CCTV cameras being used in the surveillance of UK citizens and tourists back in 2008. Despite the phenomenal financial cost, the UK Home Office has reported that street lighting is seven times more effective in preventing crime.

Not only is CCTV used in public places, it is used to promote safety and control crime on private property. Companies use it to keep an eye on employees during work hours, to combat theft and industrial espionage. We live in an environment not unlike that described by George Orwell in his book, '1984.' Computer technologies have created a daily environment far more threatening than he ever envisaged.

Micro-technology

Virtually invisible pinhole cameras with infra-red readings and cameras with recording devices hidden in mobile phones are being used ever more widely to hear and see what goes on in private conversations, along with remote monitoring devices and micro-transmitters. The miniaturization of cameras, microphones and recording devices has stolen what was left of our privacy. By trying to guard our privacy by using software on our computers, we're simply alerting intelligence agencies that we have something to hide.

Credit cards

The magnetic strip on a credit card will one day be replaced with an RFID chip, capable of storing millions of times more digital information about the card owner. With details unique to the individual, a secure smart card would be virtually immune to counterfeiting or attacks by hackers. While there are benefits, the smart card would make it possible for government, police and intelligence agencies to track our activities, our communications, our financial transactions and status, and our location at any given point in time.

Data protection

There are regulations restricting the use of data, but in reality the attacks on our personal security are overwhelming the limits that are in place.

What about encryption?

To safe-guard high-security communications, between governments, for example, highly complex and expensive encryption systems have been in place for decades. But it came to light fairly recently that throughout the years of the cold war, NSA (National Security Agency), the largest intelligence agency in the world, had secretly embedded a decryption key within the cipher text. This rendered the secret messages from most of the world's governments and large international corporations as easy to read as any ordinary open message. This development on a global scale is an indication of the way in which governments will have all their secrecy removed in the days leading up to the final events of the Tribulation, when the Anti-Christ will use the information to fuel the final global conflict.

The internet

Unbeknown to the majority, personal and business emails, even deleted ones, can be intercepted and used against an individual or company. Many internet service providers (ISPs) share our so-called private messages with law enforcement agencies around the world. NSA and police computers look for keywords, addresses, names, images, voices and numeric sequences, which not only violate our privacy but can also be used pejoratively.

Bruce Schneier, a consultant on computer encryption wrote in 'The Electronic Privacy Papers':

The odd thing is, we perceive the Net as a conversation and not as public record, and it turns out to be public record to a larger extent than people are aware of . . .you can easily imagine in 20 years a candidate being asked about a conversation he had in a chat room while he was in college. We're becoming a world where everything is recorded.

By the early 1990s the Internet had become the largest communications system in history. We're all increasingly dependent on it, and that makes it easy for intelligence agencies to monitor billions of communications every day as they search for a specific target or type of communication.

Today, every new website has to be registered, and in the US one company has sole control of all registrations. This exclusive arrangement implies full control by that company. There are checks and balances in place to provide a measure of confidence that major privacy violations will be limited. But if a future dictatorial government were to take over, it would be almost impossible to escape the control of totalitarian police, since every email, chat room conversation, web search and other internet communications can be analysed by intelligence authorities.

Google

The Google search engine alone enables more than 330 million searches daily. Google has stated that it stores its users email messages and the history of its customer's Internet searches for 18 months. Google probably has a pretty good picture of the life, health, finances, reading interests, political and religious interests, relationships and employment of each of us right now.

The Internet is a virtually indispensible tool for research, business and communication these days. We use it to keep in touch with friends, family and colleagues, for research, for making purchases, etc. It's not hard to imagine, however, what would happen if it came into the control of a global evil dictator. This could happen in the days before Jesus' return, as Revelation 13:16 implies.

RFID chips

A radio frequency identification chip (RFID) is implanted in billions of individual consumer products without our knowledge, enabling the retailer, manufacturer or intelligence agency to track the product (and the purchaser) within a certain distance of the device. At the heart of the RFID system is the Electronic Product Code (EPC) which identifies every individual item manufactured in any nation in the world, down to the most trivial items imaginable.

By 2004 more than 60,000 US corporations were putting RFID chips into every item they manufactured and distributed globally. They claim theft and fraud is drastically reduced. Libraries use RFID to track and recover lost books. Scanners can be hidden virtually anywhere and technology is improving so that soon RFID will be read even by satellite. IBM, an early promoter of RFID, has admitted:

The widespread use of RFID tags on merchandise such as clothing would make it possible for the locations of people, animals and objects to be tracked on a global scale – a privacy invasion of Orwellian proportions.

Depending on who gains access to the information provided by a RCID chip, we could all be secretly monitored in all our personal activities by unknown agencies.

Multi-application RFID cards

A single card which incorporated credit/debit card, driver's licence, car registration, insurances, prepaid travel card, medical card, etc has the advantage that it would provide a higher level of security than individual personal documents. Indeed, smart cards are being used in some form in many parts of the world, replacing cash if not other items.

Today about 97% of financial transactions globally are cashless, and the figure is set to rise as people become more comfortable with smart cards. But cards greatly endanger our privacy. The sophisticated smart card may protect us from traditional forms of fraud but a successful hacker would have access to vast amounts of confidential information. Illegal information, as well as endangering the individual, could also be used to target political or religious groups.

If you decide to avoid the dangers by using only cash, be aware that both Japan and the EU have proposed adding RFID chips to their new currency so banknotes can be tracked.

Mobile phones

Mobile phones are so common these days it's hard to imagine how we lived without them. Many people use them exclusively, and no longer have a landline in their home. Phones at the top end of the market now have an RFID chip allowing phone users to buy consumer products by holding the RFID-equipped telephone near the store's cash register, which is linked to their credit/debit card. This labour-saving device will, however, accelerate the invasion of our privacy. Any smart phone can be tracked.

Passports

RFID chips are embedded in all modern UK passports (plus other nations) enabling immigration and customs officers to process the entry of passengers into the country more efficiently. Again, the chip allows each passenger to be tracked.

ID cards

In order to avoid illegal immigration, from time to time our government calls for ID cards. Another benefit of the ID card is helping to guard against benefit fraud. Eventually, a uniform national ID card could replace identification papers including passports, licences, birth certificates, etc. A smart card with a unique ID number is the likely way it would be implemented.

The Associate Director of the Auto-ID Center, a major promoter of the universal commercial adoption of RFID technology says:

The Auto-ID Center has a clear vision – to create a world where every object – from jumbo jets to sewing needles – is linked to the Internet. Compelling as this vision is, it is only achievable if the center's system is adopted by everyone elsewhere. Success will be nothing less than global adoption.

The philosopher C P Snow remarked in an article in the New York Times back in 1971:

Technology . . . is a queer thing. It brings you great gifts with one hand, and it stabs you in the back with the other.

It isn't much of a leap to see that smart cards could be replaced by a micro-chip implanted under people's skin. This mark would remove all privacy from the individual and be the means of buying and selling. Perhaps the fact that such a thing is not inconceivable is an indication that we live in the End-Times when John foresaw individuals being completely robbed of their freedom and unable to buy or sell without the 'mark of the Beast' (Revelation 13:17-18).

A TIME TO WAKE UP!

We live in unprecedented times, a time for preparation for battle, not for business as usual! We've entered a new season in salvation history, when events will culminate in the return of Jesus Christ, a glorious prospect for the Church. Right now, events are accelerating and coming into sharper focus. Jesus may come back within the lifetime of people alive today.

All around us, we see an unparalleled escalation in world-wide ethnic cleansing and sectarian violence, increasing globalisation and a developing New World Order with a corresponding loss of national sovereignty. We see worldwide financial and economic chaos, and an increase in natural disasters. Judaeo-Christian values have been rejected here in the West and there's increasing persecution of Christians worldwide. Israel has been betrayed by her friends, and she's hemmed in on every side by enemies seeking her annihilation. We see growing apostasy in the Church, believers abandoning the true faith, and at the same time a significant growth in New Age, Eastern mysticism and pagan spirituality, promoting the deification of man and the worship of creation.

From any perspective, this is a sobering state of affairs. Dark forces of evil, in order to cover their tracks, say 'Peace, peace, when there is no peace' and scoffers rise to say 'where is the promise of his coming.' The prophets, on the other hand, recognise that we are witnessing the beginning of birth pains.

Taken together, these things lead us to the conviction that we've reached God's End Game (God's final judgements coming upon the earth). It may not be too long before we experience even more cataclysmic and earth-shattering events. But far from being 'prophets of doom', we carry with us a great sense of anticipation, expectation and urgency 'as we look forward to the day of the Lord to speed its coming' (2 Peter 3:12).

Not all Christians look at life this way, however. While storm clouds gather on national and global fronts, large sections of the Church appear to sleep whilst apostasy takes hold. As the End-Time battle for the souls of men intensifies and all hell is beginning to break loose, the Church should be experiencing her finest hour. Instead, many saints have abandoned their posts, gone absent without leave, and are hardly distinguishable now from the rest of the world. The unity that Jesus prayed for is still a distant dream.

God is given a makeover in the house of his friends. A new, softer, more palatable and culturally acceptable God - a God (or is it a goddess?) made in their own image, is now on offer. The offence of the Cross and the notions of sin, hell and judgement have been removed from the Gospel message.

Overwhelmed by the opposition, some Christians have retreated from the public square. They've given up the fight against the cruelties of abortion, the normalising of homosexuality and the rejection of our Judaeo-Christian heritage. Others embrace Paganism, New Age teaching and Eastern mysticism and inevitably drift toward the so-called 'new spirituality' of experience, relativism and tolerance.

Thankfully, it's not all bad news! In every generation, God always has a faithful remnant and we still rejoice that many come to faith each day. We can still point to faithful believers who contend for the truth of the Gospel, to vibrant communities of faith and to societies experiencing transformation through the power of the Gospel.

Nevertheless, if we take an overview, we have to admit that the Church in general has ceased to be a prophetic, subversive and counter-cultural movement – the hallmarks of the Church birthed by the Holy Spirit in the first century. And if the Church is ever to rediscover her true destiny, she first needs herself to be awakened!

In the meantime, the Lord calls his faithful remnant to battle readiness. He's raising men and women with the anointing of the men of Issachar (1 Ch 12:32), the strategists in David's army of whom it's said, 'could understand the times and knew what Israel should do.' Winston Churchill, a man for his time, used by God to deliver the world from the tyrannies of Nazi Germany, had this same anointing and calling on his life.

Today, God looks for those who will stand in the gap. Men and women, who not only understand the times and know what to do, but who also crucially understand the nature of the battle we face. Our war is not against flesh and blood, but against the rulers, against the authorities, against the powers of this dark world and against the spiritual forces of evil in the heavenly realms (Eph 6:12).

They understand that unseen forces are at work behind every philosophy, ideology and every earthly event. Like the prophet Elisha, the unseen realm is becoming as real as the seen. These people also carry a sense of urgency, knowing that as God's judgement fall, it may not be long before genuine persecution kicks in, and the politically correct State, underpinned by the spiritual forces of evil in the heavenly realms (Eph 6:12), will close down our witness for Christ.

Though the days ahead will be filled with uncertainty, and no doubt the battle will be hard, these sons and daughters of Issachar will refuse to take the easy path of appeasement and compromise.

They will declare Christ's Lordship over the powers in heavenly places (Eph 3:10) and announce to all forms of earthly government and power, that they are not sovereign. No, Jesus is Lord!

They will not give their allegiance to any human ruler or institution, nor passively submit to ungodly laws or let injustice go unchallenged. But rather, through their understanding of the times and by their example of faithfulness, they will encourage those with the spirit of prophets like Amos and Wilberforce, to go and highlight injustice, change public opinion, affect government policy and ensure continued freedom for the Gospel. As Paul urged Timothy, they will pray that we may live peaceful and quiet lives (1 Tim 2:2) where the Gospel can be proclaimed and demonstrated in every street, without limitation, and without police interference.

Equally, they will empower those with the spirit of a Wesley or Booth, to go and preach the one true Gospel, in order to see individuals, neighbourhoods, villages, towns and cities cleansed and transformed by the power of the Spirit and through the love of Jesus Christ, while there is still time. Through their purity of heart refined in the battle, they will awaken the warrior Bride, pure and spotless, clothed in white linen, made ready for the coming Bridegroom King.

Every true believer in Jesus Christ has been called for such a time as this. It's a time to let our light shine and to push back the powers of darkness, so that once again the glorious Gospel of Jesus Christ will cause an unstoppable fire to be lit in these islands of ours. The warrior Bride of Christ will become more assertive and bold, even as the battle intensifies, and as the day of her Bridegroom King's return draws ever nearer.

BIBLIOGRAPHY

Chapter 1: The New Babel

Unger, Merrill F., and Harrison, R. K.. The New Unger's Bible Dictionary. United States, Moody Publishers, 2009.

H. Edward Rowe, New Age Globalism: Humanist Agenda for Building a New World Without God. Published 1985 by Growth Publishing

Paul Kurtz, Humanist Manifestos I and II. Prometheus, 1984

Fred Bruning, "The U.N. At Forty," The Courier-Journal, 1985

Alvin Toffler, The Third Wave. Mass Market, 1984

Phillip D. Butler, Parliamentarians for World Order. The Canadian Intelligence Service, Vol. 33, No. 5, May 1983

A Declaration of Interdependence: Education for a Global Community. A Summary Report of the NEA Bicentennial Program, 1976

A. Ralph Epperson, The Unseen Hand: An Introduction to the Conspiratorial View of History. Publius Press; Later Printing edition, 1985

Chapter 2: The Move Towards One World Goverment

Our Global Neighborhood: The Report of the Commission on Global Governance. Oxford University Press, U.S.A.; 1st edition, 1995

Peter Herder, Babylon: The Resurgence of History's Most Infamous City. Forerunner Publishing, 2009

David Rothkopf, Superclass: The Global Power Elite and the World They Are Making. Farrar, Straus and Giroux; First edition (March 3, 2009)

Chapter 3: Ancient Secret Societies, Bankers, World Leaders, Organizations and National and International Institutions

Jim Marrs, Rule by Secrecy: The Hidden History That Connects the Trilateral Commission, the Freemasons, and the Great Pyramids. William Morrow Paperbacks; 1st edition (April 24, 2001)

Gary H. Kah, En Route to Global Occupation. Huntington House Pub; First Thus edition (December 1, 1996)

Edith Starr Miller, Occult Theocrasy: Vol. 1. CreateSpace Independent Publishing Platform (May 13, 2009)

Chapter 4: The Contempory Move Towards One World Goverment

United Religions Initiative (www.uri.org)

Developments in the World Constitution and Parliament Association (WCPA) (www.worldparliament-gov.org)

Chapter 5: False Gospels

Lloyd Geering, The World to Come. Polebridge Pr Westar Inst; Assumed First edition (December 1, 2000)

Our Global Neighborhood: The Report of the Commission on Global Governance. Oxford University Press, U.S.A.; 1st edition, 1995

Peter R. Jones, One or Two: Seeing a World of Difference. Main Entry Editions; First edition (June 1, 2010)

Peter Jones & James Herrick, On Global Wizardry: Techniques of Pagan Spirituality and a Christian Response. Main Entry Editions; First edition (March 1, 2010)

Peter Jones, Spirit Wars: Pagan Revival in Christian America. Winepress Pub (July 1, 1997)

George Otis, Twilight Labyrinth, The: Why Does Spiritual Darkness Linger Where It Does? (Spiritual Mapping). Chosen (November 1, 1997)

Chapter 6: Foundation of America

Thomas Paine, Common Sense. Philadelphia (January, 1776)

Thomas Paine, The Crisis. Philadelphia (April 19, 1777)

Thomas Paine, Rights of Man. Britain (March 1791 and February 1792)

Thomas Paine, The Age of Reason. 1794, 1795 and 1807

Chapter 7: Washington, DC

Robert Hieronimus Ph.D. and Laura E. Cortner, Founding Fathers, Secret Societies: Freemasons, Illuminati, Rosicrucians, and the Decoding of the Great Seal. Destiny Books; 2nd Edition, Revised, Revised Edition of <i> America's Secret Destiny</i> (December 28, 2005)

Chapter 8: Surveillance Society

George Orwell, 1984. Signet Classic (January 1, 1961)

Chapter 9: A Time to Wake Up!

AFTERWORD

Here we are in January 2021, where the New World Order machine is fully operational. Starting with the COVID19 outbreak, the government overreach to restrict our freedoms, a very-questionable 2020 presidential election in America, then the censorship from "Big Tech". All these sequential events are not random, they are programmed by the globalists.

Their rule of thumb is to trigger events and worldwide "issues" then fabricate solutions that only fit in their end goal which is to make way for the Antichrist rule.

Jesus is coming back!

ABOUT THE AUTHOR

Jean-Joseph Boni

Jean-Joseph Boni is Christian Apologetic writer, author of The Clash of Worldviews, in which he depicts the clash between the godly biblical worldview against the anti-God worldview. We then are taken "captive through hollow and deceptive philosophy, which depends on human tradition and the basic principles of this world rather than on Christ" (Colossians 2:8).

FROM THE TOWER OF BABEL TO ONE WORLD GOVERNEMNT

In order for the world leader, known as the Antichrist, to rule
economically, he will need to have a method to control all financial transactions. With the rapid changes
in technology and the global acceptance of cashless transactions, the financial system is being constructed
in order for these events to take place.